195

# MOVING SUCCESSFUL_

D0700653

# MOVING
## *Successfully*

**TOM PHILBIN**

*and the Editors of*

*Consumer Reports Books*

CONSUMER REPORTS BOOKS

A Division of Consumers Union

*Yonkers, New York*

Thanks to everyone who provided information and/or advice for this book, in particular John P. Leistritz and Smokey Spangler, Paul Arpin Van Lines; Jim Petzel, Bekins Van Lines; Anthony Jenkins, Atlas International Van Lines; Ruthann Hansen, Certified Van Service, Islandia, New York; Richie Valens, United Hall-Lane, Commack, New York; Joe McCullough and James D. Cartin, New York State Department of Transportation; and Dennis Watson and Linda Mischler, Interstate Commerce Commission. Special thanks to John W. Fristoe, Chief Operations and Insurance Branch of the ICC, who vetted portions of the manuscript.

Library of Congress Cataloging-in-Publication Data

Philbin, Tom, 1934–
   Moving successfully / Tom Philbin and the editors of Consumer Reports Books.
      p.  cm.
     Includes index.
     ISBN 0-89043-536-7
     1. Moving, Household.   I. Consumer Reports Books.
II. Title.
  TX307.P46  1994
  648′.9—dc20               93-41854
                          CIP

Design by Joy Taylor

First Printing, May 1994

Manufactured in the United States of America

This book is printed on recycled paper. ♻

# Contents

*Introduction*    1

  1. Moving Preparations    5

  2. Calculating the Costs and the Savings    15

  3. Packing    29

  4. Alternative Ways to Ship    47

  5. Do-It-Yourself Moving    51

  6. Intrastate Moving    59

  7. International Moving    63

  8. Filing a Claim    71

  9. Countdown to Moving Day    79

10. Moving Day    85

Appendix A. State Moving Regulators    91

Appendix B. Addresses of Moving Companies    95

Glossary    99

*Index*    105

# Introduction

WHEN it comes to moving household goods, there is some good news as well as some bad news.

The bad news is that moving can be a perilous undertaking. John W. Fristoe, Chief Operations and Insurance Branch of the Interstate Commerce Commission (the agency that oversees interstate moves), said that the ICC averages some 3,500 to 4,000 complaints a year about moving companies. Approximately half of these complaints are related to lost or damaged goods, whereas the rest involve higher-than-anticipated charges and/or late deliveries. In addition, *Consumer Reports* disclosed in its August 1990 issue that one out of five subscribers who had made moves was dissatisfied with the way the moving company handled the job.

The news regarding intrastate moves (moves within a state) and international moves (moves between countries) is not much better, although no agency has an exact count of the number of complaints and problems.

The good news is that you needn't be one of these dissatisfied people. Moreover, since the moving industry was deregulated in 1980, moving rates on interstate moves are no longer fixed, making it possible for consumers willing to do their homework to achieve considerable savings.

In today's economy, savings are possible now more than ever before. Cost-conscious consumers—those who know how to shop around—are growing in number, and moving companies have become more willing to give the discounts and other perks that will bring business their way. Indeed, because of the intense competition, some movers have driven their industry into a sort of depression.

The goal of this book, then, is to detail how you can take advantage of opportunities and save on a household move while protecting yourself in the process. Although the focus is on interstate moves, in most instances this information also applies to intrastate moves, and can

**Table I.1 Geographical Mobility Rates: 1950–90**

| Mobility Period | Total, One-Year-Old and Over | Total Movers | Residing in the U.S. at Beginning of the Period | | | | | | | Residing Outside the U.S. at Beginning of the Period |
| | | | Total | Different House, Same County | Different County | | | | | |
| | | | | | Total | Same State | Different State | Different Region | |
| Number | | | | | | | | | | |
| 1989–90 | 242,208 | 43,381 | 41,821 | 25,726 | 16,094 | 8,061 | 8,033 | 3,761 | 1,560 |
| 1985–86 | 232,998 | 43,237 | 42,037 | 26,401 | 15,636 | 8,665 | 6,971 | 3,778 | 1,200 |
| 1980–81 | 221,641 | 38,200 | 36,887 | 23,097 | 13,789 | 7,614 | 6,175 | 3,363 | 1,313 |
| 1975–76 | 208,069 | 36,793 | 35,645 | 22,399 | 13,246 | 7,106 | 6,140 | 3,279 | 1,148 |
| 1970–71 | 201,506 | 37,705 | 36,161 | 23,018 | 13,143 | 6,197 | 6,946 | 3,936 | 1,544 |
| 1965–66 | 190,242 | 37,586 | 36,703 | 24,165 | 12,538 | 6,275 | 6,263 | 3,348 | 883 |
| 1960–61 | 177,354 | 36,533 | 35,535 | 24,289 | 11,246 | 5,493 | 5,753 | 3,097 | 998 |
| 1955–56 | 161,497 | 34,040 | 33,098 | 22,186 | 10,912 | 5,859 | 5,053 | N.A. | 942 |
| 1950–51 | 148,400 | 31,464 | 31,158 | 20,694 | 10,464 | 5,276 | 5,188 | N.A. | 306 |
| Percent | | | | | | | | | | |
| 1989–90 | 100.0 | 17.9 | 17.3 | 10.6 | 6.6 | 3.3 | 3.3 | 1.6 | 0.6 |
| 1985–86 | 100.0 | 18.6 | 18.0 | 11.3 | 6.7 | 3.7 | 3.0 | 1.6 | 0.5 |
| 1980–81 | 100.0 | 17.2 | 16.6 | 10.4 | 6.2 | 3.4 | 2.8 | 1.5 | 0.6 |
| 1975–76 | 100.0 | 17.7 | 17.1 | 10.8 | 6.4 | 3.4 | 3.0 | 1.6 | 0.6 |
| 1970–71 | 100.0 | 18.7 | 17.9 | 11.4 | 6.5 | 3.1 | 3.4 | 2.0 | 0.8 |
| 1965–66 | 100.0 | 19.8 | 19.3 | 12.7 | 6.6 | 3.3 | 3.3 | 1.8 | 0.5 |
| 1960–61 | 100.0 | 20.6 | 20.0 | 13.7 | 6.3 | 3.1 | 3.2 | 1.7 | 0.6 |
| 1955–56 | 100.0 | 21.1 | 20.5 | 13.7 | 6.8 | 3.6 | 3.1 | N.A. | 0.6 |
| 1950–51 | 100.0 | 21.2 | 21.0 | 13.9 | 7.1 | 3.6 | 3.5 | N.A. | 0.2 |

N.A. = Not available

*Source:* U.S. Department of Commerce

help make for a smoother international move as well. For more specifics, however, see chapter 6 for information on intrastate moves and chapter 7 for advice on international moves.

## DO IT YOURSELF

Another way to save is to do it yourself. According to a study done by Ryder Transportation Resources, consumers who move themselves can save from 30 to 80 percent of the costs a professional would charge, depending on the moving distance. For example, a typical mover charges around $1,300 for a 500-mile move. Renting a truck and doing it yourself could cost around $600. Of course, there are other costs that can bring the savings down, but you can still benefit from a self-moving job.

Savings can also be achieved by doing *some* of the moving tasks yourself and letting the professionals do what you don't have the time, energy, or expertise to do.

Packing your own goods, for example, is a prime area in which to save money. According to the tariff worksheet of one nationwide mover, Mayflower Transit, a standard dish pack (a box designed specifically for packing dishes) costs $15.05. To pack one, however, the company charges $32.25. That's $47.30 for packing only one box of dishes.

In addition, suppose you need a different-size box. A 1½-cubic-foot carton from the same mover would cost you $3.20, plus $8.25 to pack it. But if you supply your own box and pack it yourself, you save $11.45. Such packing, if done professionally, can cost even more if the movers have to work overtime.

## INSURANCE

Another way to save is to purchase insurance. Therefore, if your household goods do not arrive at their destination in good condition, you will not lose out. As detailed in the *Consumer Reports* article and confirmed by professionals in the industry, damage and loss of property are more than occasional problems. You can make matters worse if you are inadequately insured or don't understand what kind of protection you are buying. Indeed, what moving companies offer is not true insurance (see chapter 2).

This book will show you how to insure your household goods—both ordinary items and what moving companies call items of ''extraordinary value'' (such as antiques, art, computer hardware, tapestries)—and how to determine the amount of money you should spend to get adequate protection.

## OTHER CONSIDERATIONS

In addition to cost and insurance, another important consideration is the impact of moving from one location to another. This can be upsetting for all of us, but it can be nothing short of traumatic for youngsters. It's not easy to be taken from a warm, safe place and transported to an unfamiliar one. Certainly, part of the experience can be exciting and happy, but it can also be quite scary.

One way to make the move as pleasant as possible for everyone is careful planning and execution, giving yourself and your family enough time to make the move. This book is filled with tips on how to do this, including worksheets and a day-by-day rundown of what to do as moving day approaches.

## USING THIS BOOK

To get the most from this guide, we suggest that you first read the portions relevant to your move. Although you can try to establish absolute order and logic in a move, this is not always possible—one step influences another. For example, as you take stock of your household goods, you need to decide what to discard; what to sell; what to send, perhaps by an alternative shipper; and what to move yourself. Each of these is a discrete activity that will impact on your move, so you want to be familiar with each step before you begin.

After reading this book, you will discover it's possible to have a successful, virtually hassle-free, money-saving move. After all, the odds are weighted in your favor. But it takes work—work prior to the move and, to some degree, once the mover arrives at your new home. But in the end, it's work that's well worth the effort.

# 1

# Moving
# Preparations

To ENSURE as smooth a move as possible, you can do certain things to help get the process started. But before getting into the details, it is a good idea to have an overall understanding of what's involved in a move and what kind of moving company to use.

## INTRASTATE OR INTERSTATE?

As mentioned in the introduction to this book, there are three types of moves you can make: *intrastate,* or within your own state; *interstate,* which involves crossing state lines; and *international,* a move to another country.

In contracting for an interstate mover, look for a van line that has a network of agents (some agents work for van lines and for themselves) or find an independent mover who does the complete move without help from any agent or van line.

A good company may be small or large, but if it moves more than 100 shipments a year, it must have Interstate Commerce Commission (ICC) authority. Although some of the larger van lines use only their employees and equipment to complete a move (no matter how involved the move), it will usually be done with the help of affiliated agents. For example, the so-called *origin agent* may provide the truck, the loaders, and the drivers at the starting point, whereas a completely different agent, called the *destination agent,* will provide services at the ending point, including people to unload the van. But the van line will coordinate everything, including putting the package of services together to get the move done.

## WHY AGENTS EXIST

Agents are hired, first of all, because it is more economical for the business. It is easy to imagine how costly it would be for a mover to main-

## About the Moving Industry

The moving industry, which generated some $7 billion in revenue in 1991 (the most recent available statistic), is defined by the Household Goods Carriers' Bureau, a private industry voice, as having four distinct segments.

• *Van lines.* These are movers who service the public through a system of agents. The Household Goods Carriers' Bureau estimates that there are 25 van lines operating in the United States.

• *Agents of van lines.* These are independently owned companies, some 4,500 in all. They work for the van lines and on their own locally, and sometimes on their own as interstate movers; some 1,000 have "operating authority"—they are licensed to cross state lines with household goods.

• *Independent, "full-service" carriers without van line or agency affiliation.* There are about 980 independents, and they have full or limited interstate authority.

• *Owner-operators.* Sometimes called independent contractors, these individuals own their trucks and are hired by other agents, van lines, or independents to load, carry, and unload goods. It is estimated there are 40,000 owner-operators.

The breakdown of the markets served by the moving industry is as follows:

### Table 1.1 Moving Industry Market

| | Percentage of Shipments | Percentage of Revenues | Average Size (Pounds) | Average Distance (Miles) |
|---|---|---|---|---|
| Household moves | | | | |
| National account (corporate) | 20.9 | 35.9 | 8,831 | 1,041 |
| Private transferee (COD shipper) | 22.1 | 26.8 | 5,435 | 1,250 |
| Government—civilian | 1.6 | 2.2 | 6,964 | 1,170 |
| Government—military | 8.9 | 9.3 | 5,256 | 1,279 |
| Total household moves | 53.5 | 74.2 | 6,775 | 1,171 |
| Second-proviso traffic | | | | |
| Office moves | 0.9 | 1.2 | 7,957 | 910 |
| Third-proviso traffic | | | | |
| Displays and exhibits | 6.6 | 6.8 | 8,553 | 1,281 |
| Electronics and other | 39.0 | 17.8 | 3,125 | 1,215 |
| Total third proviso | 45.6 | 24.6 | 5,839 | 1,248 |
| Total—all traffic | 100.0 | 100.0 | 5,478 | 1,193 |

*Source:* Household Goods Carriers' Bureau, 1991

The household goods markets account for only 54 percent of the industry's shipments, but they generate 74 percent of its revenues. Movement of electronic and trade-show shipments accounts for 46 percent of shipments and 25 percent of the revenue. Office moves account for only a small percentage of the traffic, because most such moves are local.

tain an all-company network of employees in the thousands of towns across America.

Additionally, movers have to deal with something known as *deadheading*. If a van line moves you from New York to California, it also has to bring the truck back to New York. If the mover doesn't have a load (or loads) coming back from California, it will be deadheading, or not making any money for the trip back.

On the other hand, if the van line has a network of affiliated agents in place, it is better able to fill a truck for the trip back.

## AUTHORITY TO MOVE GOODS

Although there are agents who move household goods across state lines, they may not have ICC authority (i.e., they may move less than 100 shipments a year). Therefore, these agents operate under the authority granted to the van line, and it is the van line that is responsible for the move. It must ensure that the agents abide by ICC rules and handle complaints and claims.

In order for the van line to be responsible, however, the agent must first "register" the move with the van line.

## BEST TIMES TO MOVE

One of the first decisions you'll want to make is picking the best time to move. Unless you are locked into a summer move, which the industry defines as the middle of May to the end of September, try not to move during this period. These are peak times for movers (many people want to move after their kids finish the school year), and they inflate their rates accordingly (an average of 10 percent). In addition, you can expect to pay overtime charges if you move on a holiday or on a weekend. Whatever the sea-

son, though, the best time to move is during the beginning or middle of the month; the end of the month is generally the worst—everyone wants that time.

### Summer Months

Depending on your individual circumstances, it may be possible to move during the summer months and not pay fattened rates. If you get a binding bid from a mover (see chapter 2), the price will normally be good for 60 days. So if you sign up in May—say, May 12—you have until July 12 to move at the original price.

## SELECTING A MOVER: FIRST STEPS

In selecting a mover, it is important to remember one thing: Any company you are thinking of hiring—whether it's a large outfit or a small one—must be evaluated on its own merits, not on the reputation of an affiliated company. Van lines, particularly large van lines, have many different agents working for them—some good and some not as good. You can't rely on the van lines to protect you from harm.

### Give Yourself Some Time

It may require six to eight weeks to select a mover. This time is needed not only to find potentially good movers but also to take bids, which is the way to save money.

### Start with a List

To select a mover, make a list of movers by consulting with people who have recently moved: friends, relatives, business acquaintances. Perhaps the real estate agent helping to sell your house or your insurance agent can provide some names. Or, if possible, consult with the traffic manager of a big company. Such individuals deal with movers all the time and should know which movers are reliable.

Neighbors—for example, the family down the block that recently moved in—may also provide you with a good recommendation. Neighbors are usually happy to talk about consumer-related matters. We've all been chiseled, and most people are inclined to dispense free help and advice to save others from a similar experience.

You should strive for a list of four or five "good" movers, then check their standing with the regional office or main office of the ICC in Washington, D.C. (see box on page 10). Look for the following:

1. Whether a particular mover has "authority on file." This means that the ICC allows the mover to be a common carrier and to move goods across state lines. If the mover is an agent for a van line, then the agent would give the van line's ICC number.

Assuming the authority is there, also ask what the mover's motor carrier (MC) number is and whether it is *active*. If the ICC has no record of the mover, or the mover's number isn't active, don't give the company any further consideration. It means the mover is not authorized to carry goods.

In their advertisements, including the ones listed in the telephone book, the interstate mover is required to print the MC number of the authority performing the move. If it's not there, question why.

2. Whether the mover has insurance on file. To get this information, you must have the MC number. Ask if the mover has active cargo, bodily injury, and property damage insurance.

3. Tariff on file. For movers that have common carrier authority, a copy of their rules and rates, known as *tariffs*, must be filed with the ICC.

## Complaints

You should also check for complaints about the companies with the department of consumer affairs in your area. If the company operates intrastate, chances are you can also get information from the state transportation department or public utilities commission. (The type of information can vary from state to state.)

When checking with consumer affairs departments, contact the office in the home area of a particular company. For example, if you are hiring an Erie, Pennsylvania, company and you live in New York State, by all means check with consumer affairs officials in Erie.

Remember, too, that some complaints may be unresolved and that there are two sides to every story. However, a pattern of many complaints should send up a red flag.

## Visiting the Mover

Try making an unannounced visit to the mover's place of business and ask for a grand tour. Then determine how the company looks. Are things neat, clean, orderly? Or does it look disorganized and chaotic?

What about the mover's trucks? Do they seem well maintained? Do they look sturdy enough to transport your goods? Is this the kind of outfit that you want moving practically everything you own in the world?

## Performance Reports

The ICC also gathers "performance reports" on larger interstate companies (over 100 moves a year), and these companies are required to give you a copy of their report when they come to your house for an estimate. The report lists on-time performance on pickup and delivery. However, if the company you're thinking of using is just an agent for a van line, you may not learn anything about individual performance data.

The figures may be lumped together with those of other agents under the van line's name. Furthermore, the authenticity of the performance data is suspect because they are actually compiled by the companies. The ICC doesn't require proof of claims, nor does it impose penalties for twisting the truth a bit.

Still, the reports may have some value. Some companies appear to be telling the truth (the data do not always make them look good), and all companies reporting are licensed, insured, and under ICC auspices, which lends some credibility to the report. This is especially true in view of the questions the ICC asks movers.

The following table contains the names of the companies with the greatest number of moves and their performance reports as filed with the ICC. If one of these movers is close to you, you might want to consider it.

## Table 1.2 Performance Reports for Companies with at Least 20,000 Moves (1991)

| Moving Company | Private Shipments | Government (Military) Shipments | Commercial Shipments | Accuracy of Estimate* | On-Time Pickup Rate† | On-Time Delivery Rate‡ | Damage-Free Moves§ |
|---|---|---|---|---|---|---|---|
| Allied Van Lines | 63,478 | 11,196 | 81,059 | 81 | 97.9 | 96.8 | 96 |
| American Red Ball Transit | 3,945 | 4,876 | 16,563 | 93 | 99.7 | 95.7 | 91.3 |
| Paul Arpin Van Lines | 8,582 | 5,347 | 11,030 | 97.7 | 100 | 98 | 97.4 |
| Atlas Van Lines | 17,513 | 6,176 | 45,054 | 99 | 99.4 | 99.7 | 97 |
| Bekins Van Lines | 29,868 | 6,203 | 22,466 | 98.5 | 99.7 | 98.1 | 94 |
| Global Van Lines | 6,699 | 7,258 | 13,166 | 96.2 | 99.3 | 98.4 | 96.1 |
| Graebel Van Lines | 1,842 | 2,993 | 20,804 | 75.1 | 99.9 | 99.3 | 98.4 |
| Mayflower Transit, Inc. | 41,906 | 8,235 | 40,251 | 60.7 | 98.7 | 98.4 | 98.5 |
| National Van Lines, Inc. | 4,942 | 14,412 | 2,011 | 90.1 | 99.1 | 97.3 | 97.6 |
| North American Van Lines | 53,637 | 17,691 | 48,668 | 50 | 98 | 94 | 95 |
| United Van Lines | 51,743 | 17,324 | 81,616 | 67.8 | 99.3 | 95.6 | 95.3 |
| Wheaton Van Lines | 7,819 | 5,962 | 6,270 | 93 | 99 | 98.1 | 98 |

*Percentage of shipments whose final charge did not exceed the estimate (nonbinding estimates only).
†Percentage of shipments that were picked up on or before the last date specified on the order for service/bill of lading.
‡Percentage of shipments that were delivered on or before the last date specified on the order for service/bill of lading.
§Percentage of shipments delivered that did not result in the filing of a claim by the shipper for property loss or damage in excess of $100 within 60 days following the date of delivery.

*Source:* Interstate Commerce Commission

## Two Important Questions

In selecting any company, there are two important questions to ask:

1. Will my belongings be on one truck for the entire move?

2. Are the people who will do the packing and unpacking—at origin and destination—trained for the job?

The first question is important because household goods are not designed to be moved, and the less they're moved, the better their chances of not being damaged. If they have to be switched from one truck to another, you're increasing the likelihood for damage.

The second question is important, too, because not every worker who participates in a move is necessarily a good packer. Packing is something that requires training, and if your goods are packed or loaded incorrectly, you can be sure they'll be damaged. In the average household move, a worker goes back and forth carrying goods between truck and house over 200 times!

## Contacting the ICC

To verify whether a mover has the authority to make moves and/or has insurance, you can contact one of the following regional offices of the ICC's Office of Compliance and Consumer Assistance (OCCA):

• Room 16400, 3535 Market Street, Philadelphia, PA 19104, 215-596-4040.

• Suite 550, 55 West Monroe Street, Chicago, IL 60603, 312-353-6204.

• Suite 500, 211 Main Street, San Francisco, CA 94105, 415-744-6520.

OCCA's headquarters are in Room 4133, ICC Building, 12th Street and Constitution Avenue NW, Washington, DC 20423, 202-927-5520.

Remember to get the mover's MC number before you contact the ICC.

In other words, you don't want your goods packed or loaded by helpers who are inexperienced or not properly trained. This is one more reason to avoid the summer months if you can. When overwhelmed with orders, movers may hire people who have little or no experience in moving.

## Bigger Company May Be Better

In the moving industry, a "local" move generally involves a total distance of under 500 miles. Anything over that is considered "long distance." Therefore, on a longer move it may be better to stay with one of the major van lines. They are much more likely to have a network of well-trained people in place who can handle your move. Let's say you hire the local, independent ABC Movers for a move to Whitefish, Montana. ABC may be able to get good people involved in the move at the origin, but what about the destination? Will your mover have good helpers there to unload?

If you hire one of the big movers, it's more likely they can bring in people who can do a professional packing and unloading job—and they will have the necessary equipment to make a move of any length.

## Final Selection

Try to get bids from at least three companies before you choose. But how do you do this? There is no magic formula for picking the best mover for you, but if a company doesn't have a history of complaints, its facilities and equipment look good, it is registered and insured with the ICC, it keeps goods on one truck for the entire move, and it can provide trained people at origin and destination, then all you have to do is decide on the best price.

Price alone should never be the sole criterion for choosing a company. All the factors mentioned above should be considered before you make your decision.

*Tip:* Whomever you pick, make sure that everything is in writing. It avoids misunderstanding and heartache later on.

# CHOOSING AN INTRASTATE OR INTERNATIONAL MOVER

Selecting an intrastate or international mover is different, to some degree, from selecting an interstate mover because intrastate moves are not regulated by the ICC (although there is monitoring in some states). The ICC also doesn't regulate international moves. To choose one of these movers, you can use the steps discussed previously, but there are some important variations, as detailed in chapters 6 and 7.

# OTHER CONSIDERATIONS

Moves also include shutting down or canceling services at your old address. To ensure a smooth, uninterrupted flow of mail to your new address, notify the post office when you will be moving and what your new address will be. In some cases, you may not know this yet, but you should at least give the post office a temporary address—say, a post office box. If you want a P.O. box, you must open it in person; rentals are usually for a minimum of six months and cost about $17 for a small box, which you pay up front. If you need an address for only a month or two, you may want to opt for something else, such as your new employer's address or the address of a business acquaintance, family member, or friend.

### Change-of-Address Cards

To get mail shipped to the new address will require that you fill out a change-of-address card, something you can pick up at any post office. Or you can call the post office and ask to have a carrier drop the cards off with the mail. One card is required for each person with a different last name who will reside at the new address.

### Notify All Concerned Parties

Listed here are the many businesses and other concerns that must be notified of your move. In each case, six to eight weeks' prior notice should be given. (Additional information on this subject appears in chapter 9.)

• *Utilities:* water, gas, electricity, fuel, trash, sewer, cable.

*Tip:* If you contact the utility companies in your new city early enough, it may well be possible to have service turned on before you arrive.

• *Insurance agencies:* life, health, automobile, homeowner's.

• *Professional services:* doctor, dentist, accountant, lawyer, stockbroker. Once you are established in your new home, ask your doctor or dentist to refer you to a physician in your new location.

• *Regular business accounts:* landscaping service, milk delivery, bakery, diaper service, water-softening service, car repair service, laundry, finance company, credit card company, road service, bank, department store, drugstore, dry cleaner.

• *Governmental agencies:* Social Security, state department of motor vehicles, IRS, state tax bureau, land assessor, draft board.

• *Magazine, newspaper, or newsletter publishers.* They usually need to be notified as soon as possible. Some publishers require at least six weeks' prior notice to ensure uninterrupted service. This is also the time to notify them of any subscriptions you wish to cancel.

### Eliminate What You Don't Need

As will be explained in chapter 3, one of the prime ways to save money on a move is by generally eliminating all items you don't need.

Six to eight weeks before the big day, start disposing of food that would otherwise go to waste. Start using up canned goods and frozen foods. If you are not traveling over 150 miles and the move will be completed within 24 hours, it may be practical to take frozen foods with you.

Household items such as paper goods, cleaning supplies, and anything flammable should be used, given away, or disposed of. (Loading flammable materials in a moving truck is against the law.)

## Other Items

Other items that may be thrown out or given away include old clothing, toys, furniture, and just about anything you figure you won't need at the new location. One good way to dispose of such items is to give them to charitable organizations, but get a receipt showing the value of the items for possible tax deductions. Another way is to hold a garage sale (see box below).

## Be Ruthless but Careful

In disposing of possessions before a move, there are two important rules: (1) Be as ruthless as you can be, but (2) take care when it comes to disposing of the belongings of other family members.

Sometimes it is hard to be ruthless (the purpose of discarding items is not to engage in a throwaway frenzy). But just ask yourself this: How long has the item I want to throw out been around, and is it still useful? If your answer is

---

## Running a Successful Garage Sale

A garage sale is a great way to dispose of unwanted articles and to receive money for them in the process. The following tips can help make your garage sale a success:

• Advertise it well. Place an ad in the local "pennysaver," or wherever garage-sale mavens look. If you have a preponderance of one or more items, such as tools or toys, by all means list these in the ad.

• Make easy-to-read signs detailing the date, time, and location of the sale, then tack them up in your neighborhood on or before the day of the sale.

• Research prices of items to be sold at the garage sale a couple of weeks before the actual date. Don't be greedy—price items so they sell. Receiving 50 cents for an item is better than never receiving $2.00.

• Clean, wash, and spruce up the sale items as needed before setting them out. A clean glass will sell better than a dirty one.

• Use stick-on labels to indicate prices.

• If you have a cluster of things at one price—for example, 25 cents—place them all together with a single sign.

• Place all books and records on tables where they can be reached easily. Most people dislike bending down and foraging through boxes, which is how sellers commonly display them. Also, arrange containers so titles can be read as easily as possible.

• Hang clothing on hangers.

• Keep a sharp eye on valuable items such as jewelry, coins, etc. Shoplifting is quite common at garage sales. Also, keep the sales receipts in a safe place.

• If you have things for sale inside the house, post a sign announcing this. (To prevent theft, make sure that you—or a friend or relative—accompany anyone going into your home.)

• When you sell furniture, try not to break up a set. If someone wants just one item in a set, tell him or her to come back later. If the set hasn't been sold, then the buyer can purchase the individual item.

• Be prepared to negotiate prices on bigger items. Remember, the goal is to sell items you would otherwise be forced to discard.

"years" and that it hasn't been useful, you know where the item belongs.

As far as being careful with the property of family members, that simply means you shouldn't indiscriminately dispose of their belongings. That battered teddy bear that may look valueless to you can be very meaningful to your son or daughter.

## Designate a Central Place

It's a good idea to ask first before discarding someone else's possessions. In fact, it's a better idea to designate a central place in the home where questionable items can be deposited until other family members can make a decision about them. As you collect these items, earmark a storage closet for the ones that definitely will be taken.

To help decide what to keep and what to dispose of, make an inventory of your possessions. As detailed in chapter 8, it is essential to have written, photographic, or other proof of what you own to support any claims you may have for damaged or missing goods.

## Who Moves?

There is no question that Americans are among the most mobile people in the world. According to the most recent data from the U.S. Census Bureau, 94 million Americans moved into new homes during the 12 months prior to the last half of 1989. The 1990 census also revealed a variety of other facts:

• Renters are four times more likely to have moved than property owners.

• About 56 percent of recent movers (those who moved within the 12 months prior to the census survey) stayed in the same metropolitan area. Another 19 percent moved from one metropolitan area to another. About 14 percent remained in a nonmetropolitan area, usually within the same state. Nine percent moved from a nonmetropolitan area, or vice versa. Two percent moved to the United States from another country.

• The most mobile region was the West; about one in four households were recent movers. Next was the South at 20 percent and the Midwest at 12 percent.

• Movers were younger than nonmovers. The median age for homeowners who moved during the previous 12 months was 37 years. This compares to 52 years for owners who had lived in their homes for at least 12 months. Among renters, the median age for movers and nonmovers was 31 and 41 years, respectively.

• Moving rates declined with age. Among homeowners, moving rates ranged from 28 percent for householders under age 30 to 2 percent for those 65 years of age and over.

For renters, the proportion that moved during the past year ranged from 56 percent for householders under age 30 to 12 percent for those 65 years of age and older.

• Movers lived in newer housing than nonmovers did. Homes occupied by recent movers had a median age of 14 years, compared with 26 years for homes occupied by owners who hadn't moved.

• Recent movers/owners had higher incomes. Owners who moved had a median income of $37,600, or 14 percent higher than the median income of owners who hadn't moved, which was $32,900. However, the median income of renters who moved ($18,100) was not statistically different from that of renters who lived in their homes for over a year ($18,400).

• Monthly housing costs were higher for movers.

# IMPORTANT POINTS

• An interstate move is one that crosses state lines; an intrastate move stays within state boundaries; and international moves involve relocating to a different country.

• Make sure that when you are evaluating a moving company, you evaluate the company that's moving you, not the major van line affiliated with the agent.

• The cheapest time to move is during the nonsummer months. Summer months are considered to be from the middle of May to the end of September.

• Get a list of movers from credible sources, such as friends and neighbors who have used particular companies. (See the table of performance reports, page 9.) Give yourself six to eight weeks or so to do this.

• Check the names on your list with consumer affairs groups, as well as the ICC, for confirmation on movers' authority to operate, their active MC numbers, and insurance matters.

• When getting bids from movers, make sure that your shipment will stay on the original truck until its intended destination.

• Make sure the people who are going to do the loading and unloading are trained.

• Cut your costs by discarding and/or using up materials you don't need.

# 2

# Calculating the Costs and the Savings

THERE are a variety of factors that go into the cost of a move, but happily there are also a variety of ways to save.

## WEIGHT AND DISTANCE

Basically, a move is priced by weight and distance. The heavier the load and the farther it travels, the more it will cost. The Household Goods Carriers' Bureau (HGCB) is a private agency that decides moving charges based on input from member companies. These rates, along with the rules and regulations under which the companies must operate, are then published. Collectively, these rates and rules are known as *tariffs.*

Tariffs include basic charges called *line-haul charges.* In addition, there are other set charges for such things as packing, unpacking, and the like. All of these charges are also put in writing.

## MEANINGLESS RATES

In the marketplace, however, published rates are essentially meaningless. You should be able to negotiate prices down. Surveys have repeatedly shown that most companies offer discounts ranging from 10 to 50 percent and sometimes more. (To offer these rates, moving companies must apply to the ICC for a rate exception.) For example, one consumer magazine queried 10 carriers and found that rates to ship 5,000 pounds of household goods about 2,000 miles (from Minneapolis to San Antonio) varied from a low of around $1,600 to a high of $2,600—a $1,000 difference!

## CARTONS AND PACKING

Many people assume that moving companies will supply the cartons for a move, then pack and unpack them as well. Movers will do so, of course, but there are attendant charges for each service. The following are typical prices for car-tons—and what movers charge for packing and unpacking them at both straight and overtime labor rates.

| | Container | Packing | | Unpacking | |
|---|---|---|---|---|---|
| | | Regular | Overtime | Regular | Overtime |
| Dish packs | $15.05 | $32.25 | $45.15 | $10.85 | $15.20 |
| Cartons—1½ cu. ft. | 3.20 | 8.25 | 11.55 | 2.80 | 3.90 |
| Cartons—3 cu. ft. | 4.60 | 12.95 | 18.15 | 4.40 | 6.10 |
| Cartons—4½ cu. ft. | 5.50 | 15.85 | 22.20 | 5.35 | 7.45 |
| Cartons—6 cu. ft. | 6.35 | 18.05 | 25.30 | 6.10 | 8.55 |
| Cartons—6½ cu. ft. | 6.90 | 21.30 | 29.90 | 7.25 | 10.10 |
| Wardrobe carton | 11.80 | 9.45 | 13.20 | 2.05 | 2.80 |
| Crib mattress carton | 4.35 | 7.40 | 10.35 | 2.45 | 3.45 |
| Double mattress carton | 9.65 | 9.10 | 12.75 | 3.10 | 4.30 |
| Twin mattress carton | 7.80 | 9.10 | 12.75 | 3.10 | 4.30 |
| King/queen mattress carton | 15.65 | 14.40 | 20.15 | 4.80 | 6.75 |
| Long twin mattress carton | 11.00 | 9.10 | 12.75 | 3.10 | 4.30 |
| Mattress cover | 5.65 | 5.75 | 8.05 | 1.90 | 2.60 |
| Mirror carton | 12.15 | 29.45 | 41.30 | 9.95 | 13.95 |
| Minimum crates | -0- | 48.30 | 67.60 | 9.25 | 12.95 |
| Cubic foot crates | -0- | 12.05 | 16.90 | 2.30 | 3.25 |

*Source:* United Hall-Lane, March 1992 prices.

It is easy to see how buying containers and paying for packing and unpacking can balloon the cost of a move, but you can reduce that cost by supplying your own cartons and doing at least some of the packing and unpacking. (De-tails on doing it yourself are contained in chap-ter 3.)

## SPECIAL SITUATIONS

Other possible costs, depending on the partic-ulars of the move, may fall into a category called special situations. Three common ones are the *stair carry,* the *elevator carry,* and the *exces-sive-distance carry.*

• *Stair carry.* You should not be charged for

movers to climb one flight of steps within a single-family home. But any steps above the first flight do carry a charge, with the amount usually based on eight steps, each constituting a so-called stair carry.

Likewise, no charge should be assessed for a stair carry for the first flight of steps outside a building, but there will be a charge for anything after that. An outside stair-carry charge is based on 19 steps. For example, 8 to 27 steps would count as one carry charge, whereas 88 to 107 steps would count as five carry charges.

Most companies will charge by the stair carry—approximately $1.25 per 100 pounds. But some will charge more or less than that, and have their own way of figuring costs.

• *Elevator carry.* One might assume that an

elevator carry would cost less than a stair carry, but it actually costs more because it takes time to load the elevator. If the elevator is within a single-family home, there should be no charge at all. Also, if the movers have a choice between an elevator and stairs, the shipper should charge the least costly way, even if the elevator is used. The typical cost is $1.25 per 100 pounds.

*Note:* There should not be any charge based on the number of floors involved.

*Tip:* If you live in an apartment building, notify your superintendent before the move that you want to use the elevator.

• *Excessive-distance carry.* If the movers must carry your goods more than 25 yards (75 feet), it is considered an excessive-distance carry. The typical cost is $0.85 to $1.10 per 100 pounds for every 50 feet. If you live in an apartment building, you must pay for the stair carry as well as the excessive-distance carry if over 75 feet.

## BULKY ARTICLES

Extra charges will also be assessed for items that are more difficult to carry, require extra care, or are otherwise considered "special."

*Note:* If a stair carry, elevator carry, or excessive-distance carry is involved in the moving of a bulky article, these charges will be added to the bill. The following is a list of bulky articles and the typical moving cost for each item.

| | |
|---|---|
| Car | $113.05 |
| Piano, organ, or harpsichord over 38 inches high | 63.75 |
| Grandfather clock over 5 feet high | 28.30 |
| Playhouse/dollhouse/shed | 106.05 |
| Hot tub, spa, whirlpool | 106.05 |
| Tractor/mower less than 25 horsepower | 56.60 |
| Snowmobile/jet ski | 56.50 |

| | |
|---|---|
| Motorized golf cart | 56.50 |
| Utility/pop-up trailer over 14 feet | 106.05 |
| Utility/pop-up trailer less than 14 feet | 56.60 |
| Motorcycle/go-cart/ATV | 56.60 |
| Farm trailers/tractors | 176.75 |

*Source:* United Hall-Lane, March 1992 prices.

## EXTRA HELP

Included in the line-haul charge is a standard service requirement that movers deposit boxes and other items into the rooms where they belong. Movers will also normally assemble bed or crib frames.

Beyond this, it will cost extra to have more assembly done—for example, if you want your toolshed or storage shed reassembled. If this is the case, you should alert the company, since many movers will arrange to have their people do it for a regular hourly rate.

## THIRD-PARTY SERVICES

Another possible cost is what is known in the industry as *third-party services.* This refers to people hired to perform tasks that the moving company may not perform because of liability concerns or a shortage of personnel.

Typically, this would involve such things as disconnecting appliances, disassembling large pool tables (the slate and frame must be separately boxed), or taking apart the mechanism within a grandfather clock.

## YOU CAN DO IT

Anyone who is careful can get an appliance ready for shipping (movers can even supply Styrofoam wedges to block washing machine agitators), and your public utility company may also do it for you. Specialists are recommended for packing such things as grandfather clocks and pool tables. Here again, call a few people to get the best price. To find a specialist, simply call a retail establishment or company that sells the particular item being shipped. Perhaps the person who recommended the mover also knows a specialist.

## SIDE TRIPS

Another possible expense occurs when a mover has to make a side trip, either at the origin or at the destination. For example, if you have items (or one large item such as a boat) at some other location and want to pick them up on the way to your destination, this constitutes a side trip.

## Moving Company Incentives

Although many moving companies do not attempt to make themselves more attractive to consumers, some do provide what can be called "sweeteners"— products or services that give you a good feeling about a company and convince you to select them.

What follows are some of the incentives being offered today. It is suggested that when estimators come to your home, you ask them if they have any extras like the ones described here.

### Relocation Services

A number of companies offer relocation services for both national and international moves—that is, free information profiling the area you are moving to. United Van Lines' Bette Malone Relocation Service is offered to individuals as well as corporations. On interstate moves, this service provides information on climate and geography, commerce and industry, schools, shopping districts, medical facilities, places of worship, and cultural activities.

It will also research special questions for customers. For example, you may want to know where you can board a horse in your new location. Even more unusual questions get researched by the service.

For corporate moves, United Van Lines offers the same service plus a seminar on moving for the corporation's employees. There is also a seminar designed to help employees' spouses find employment.

Atlas, Paul Arpin, Bekins, and other companies also offer location information. A particularly good series of pamphlets on international moves is available from Atlas. Paul Arpin operates a moving institute that offers a toll-free number (800-343-3500)

for consumers to obtain detailed literature on the various aspects of a move. (To find out if the moving company you're interested in has a toll-free number, you can call 800-555-1212.)

American Red Ball, an interstate and international mover based in Indianapolis, offers a kit designed to make moving easier. The customer receives an envelope that contains a variety of materials: a guide to a moving sale, a cardboard "Moving Sale" sign, an assortment of gummed labels ("Fragile," "This End Up," etc.), change-of-address cards, a calendar to track the move, and lots of tips on the move itself. Truck rental companies also offer instructional literature.

A number of movers offer instructional videos on making a move. For example, Atlas offers a 12-minute video on interstate moves, and U-Haul has a video on moving yourself.

### Bonus for Selling Your Home

A sweetener offered by Allied is its plan entitled "Money on Relocation Expenses." It provides monetary incentives if you sell your existing home or buy your new home through an independent real estate agency or direct relocation service corporation. For example, you will receive a bonus of $50 per $10,000 involved in either transaction. If you sold your current home for $120,000, you'd get $600. If you bought a new home for $130,000, you'd get $650 more.

Of course, as mentioned at the beginning of this chapter, the best sweeteners of all are the moving discounts that are commonly available.

Such trips are usually not expensive, but this is something to tell the moving company about so that the price—and the details of the move—can be settled before moving day. Moving companies and/or their drivers don't mind making a side trip as long as the distance involved does not seriously interfere with their itinerary. Moving vans commonly carry three or four separate loads of household goods, and their routes are carefully laid out.

# VALUATION AND INSURANCE

Valuation and insurance, also known in the trade as ''released values''—the amounts the carrier is liable for in case of loss or damage—also add to moving costs. However, savings are possible, depending on how much and what kind of protection you purchase.

Household moves are covered in some cases by standard homeowner's insurance, but this is something to ask your insurance agent about. After considering what insurance the movers have to offer, you may prefer to rely solely on your homeowner's insurance (you can usually buy additional coverage for a move).

It's important to understand the difference between valuation and true insurance. *Valuation* is the amount of value you place on your shipment. If something is damaged or lost, you can get reimbursement or compensation, but only so long as you can prove the mover is liable.

*Insurance* is different. With insurance, you get a policy detailing what is covered and what is not, and although you have to show there has been a loss to collect any money, liability is not involved.

## Types of Valuation

Different types of valuation are available: limited liability, added valuation, lump sum, and full replacement (all of which go by different names in a particular company).

• *Limited liability.* This is free to customers but can be costly in other ways. It states that your goods are covered for only 60 cents per pound. For example, if the mover breaks an expensive statue that cost you, say, $200 but weighs only 2 pounds, you'd get only $1.20 back.

Limited liability valuation must be requested in writing. Our advice is to forget it—it's generally useless.

• *Added valuation.* Here, you can get back the replacement cost of the item—that is, its worth today after depreciation. To calculate depreciation, 10 percent of the original sale price is subtracted for each year of ownership. If the item was purchased for $100 three years ago, it would be worth $70 now.

You declare the item's worth, then pay 50 cents per $100 of the value you assign it. If you don't declare a value, then the moving company, following ICC rules, will automatically value the goods at $1.25 per pound, which can be inadequate when you factor in depreciation. Moreover, the total shipment is worth only the specific total dollar amount you declare. For example, if you declare $6,000 and the truck crashes and burns and your goods are destroyed, then $6,000 is the maximum amount you will get for them.

• *Lump sum.* A variation on the added valuation is lump-sum valuation, by which you release or value the shipment at any figure greater than $1.25 per pound. Again, you would pay 50 cents per $100 of the value, and depreciation applies.

• *Full value.* Full-value protection is just that—you pay for valuation that will pay you full price for replacing or repairing something. Under ICC rules, you must declare a minimum value of $3.50 a pound.

## Other Coverage

Some companies also offer various *full-replacement packages*, with some plans having a deductible of usually $250, $500, or $1,000 (others may have no deductible). Typically, figure on paying around 35 cents per $100 with a $250 deductible, 20 cents per $100 with a $500 deductible, and 10 cents or so per $100 with a $1,000 deductible.

Most people opt for full-replacement coverage. A deductible is of questionable value, since the average claim in the industry is around $450. Unless you're covered under your homeowner's policy, you may want to skip the deductible, pay a bit more, and be in the position of collecting 100 percent of your loss.

### Items of Extraordinary Value

If you have items of high value—those worth more than $100 per pound—alert the company estimator in order to obtain appropriate valuation. This is called "valuation of items of extraordinary value." Antiques, art, cameras, computers, firearms, furs, jewelry, manuscripts, rugs, silver, tapestries, and electronic equipment are among the items that can fall into this category. Insurance costs can be high, so many people choose to carry such items themselves.

## STORAGE CHARGES

It is estimated that one in four families who move will require temporary storage of their household goods, also known as *storage-in-transit (SIT)*. For example, your new house may not be quite ready, but school and job commitments require that you move. If so, storage is another expense to consider.

You can have your belongings placed in a warehouse affiliated with the mover or in a public warehouse. The advantage of a public warehouse is easier access to your property. If your possessions are stored in a private warehouse, they are kept in plywood containers known as vaults and are difficult to get at—even if you

need to get only one particular item, you will be assessed a fee.

On the other hand, some experts say that it is better to have your belongings in these vaults rather than having them stacked or loose on a warehouse floor.

### Private Rates

Rates for private facilities are based on 100-pound increments. If the items are stored for more than 90 days, then the SIT status ends and the possessions are considered to be in permanent storage. Usually, SIT rates are higher than permanent-storage rates, but not always.

If possible, *avoid* storing your belongings. According to a study detailed in the August 1990 issue of *Consumer Reports,* about 60 percent of all shipments placed in storage suffered some damage, compared with 39 percent when shipped direct. This is no surprise, considering the extra handling the goods are subjected to in storage.

If the mover provides the storage, you may be able to negotiate the cost down.

## SPECIAL SERVICE NEEDS

When you contract for a move, your belongings are often loaded on a truck along with the household goods of other people. But there are a number of special situations where you may have more particular needs, as follows.

• *Space reservation.* You may not know exactly how much space your belongings will require in the truck. You can reserve the cubic space, but you must pay for all of it even if your goods do not occupy all of the space.

• *Guaranteed service.* Normally, a carrier will give you a spread of a few days when you can expect your delivery. If you want a specific day, you can get it, but it costs extra.

• *Expedited service.* If you use this plan, you can have your shipment delivered on a date when the carrier normally does not operate.

• *Exclusive use of a vehicle.* If you want your goods delivered speedily, you can pay for private use of the moving truck.

*Tip:* Remember, it's more expensive to move during the summer months. Holidays and weekends are expensive, too, because you pay overtime charges.

# ADDITIONAL TRANSPORTATION CHARGES

*Additional transportation charges (ATC)* apply if a carrier faces abnormal travel obstacles, such as having to circumvent a narrow bridge or travel in city traffic. Time is money to

## Saving on Taxes

If you qualify, you may be able to deduct the cost of moving household goods and the cost of traveling to your new home from your taxable income. However, as a result of recent tax law changes, tough new limits on moving-expense deductions began in 1994. The new tax law won't allow deductions for meals, house-hunting excursions, temporary living expenses up to 30 days, and costs related to selling a home, settling an unexpired lease, or getting a new home (for example, fees paid to lenders or real estate commissions). But any costs that are not deductible can be subtracted in computing adjusted gross income. This is preferable to listing such costs as an itemized deduction. In addition, costs paid or reimbursed by the taxpayer's employer can be excluded from gross income.

In brief, you qualify for moving-expense deductions if (1) the move was made as a result of a job relocation, and you will now have to travel at least 50 additional miles to work (college students qualify if their new job location is more than 50 miles from their legal home), (2) you move within one year of starting the new job, and (3) you work at least 39 weeks out of the year after the move in the area of the new job location.

*Tip:* If you don't meet the 39-week requirement by the time taxes are due but you expect to, you can take the deduction anyway or file an amended tax form later.

### What Can You Deduct?

If you qualify, you can deduct all the expenses of the move—there is no ceiling—including such costs as

moving your car, transporting pets, insurance charges, and storage beginning 30 consecutive days after the move. All costs related to travel (except meals) can also be deducted up to 80 percent.

### New-Home Expenses

Also deductible, up to a maximum of $3,000, are expenses related to the selling of your old home, buying your new home, house hunting, temporary housing, and even the security deposit you may have lost because you had to break a lease. You should, of course, keep all your receipts related to the move.

*Note:* You may not be entitled to deductions if your employer pays for the move. Check with your tax preparer.

### Helpful Publications

The IRS provides a variety of useful free publications, including Publication 521, "Moving Expenses"; Publication 523, "Tax Information on Selling Your Home"; and Publication 530, "Tax Information for Homeowners." Also, obtain Publication 553, available each January, which contains highlights of tax changes. This way, you can make sure requirements related to moves haven't changed. To obtain any of these publications, call 800-829-3676 or write to Internal Revenue Service, Forms Distribution Center, Richmond, VA 23260.

a moving company, and if your move involves travel delays, you have to pay extra—and such costs can vary. A study by one consumer magazine noted that the ATC charge by North American Van Lines for a move to a Boston suburb was $1.55 per 100 pounds. It was only 37 cents for a move to San Antonio or Salt Lake City, and 75 cents for San Francisco.

## Surcharges

A 4 percent surcharge on the line-haul price (to cover valuation costs to companies) will be added to your bill. This extra fee is known in the industry as "item 60." Sometimes, fuel surcharges are tacked on as well.

# ESTIMATES

Getting moving costs down starts with getting companies to give estimates on a job. You can have all company representatives come on the same day (allowing two hours or so for each) or on separate days, but the important thing is to alert them that you're shopping around. You want them to come prepared to give you their best estimates. The most important question to ask them is whether their companies give discounts. If they don't, they're probably not worth dealing with, since the majority of companies do offer discounts.

## Nonbinding Estimates

Estimates fall into two general categories: nonbinding and binding. The *nonbinding,* or "weight-rated," estimate is just what the name implies: The estimator comes to your home and takes inventory of what you want moved. Then, on a standard form, the estimator writes down the services you require and gives an estimate of the combined charges.

*Note:* The actual charges often differ from the nonbinding estimate. It all depends on the ac-

tual weight of your possessions. To determine this, on moving day the empty moving van—with no one aboard, the gas tanks full, and all moving equipment loaded inside—is weighed at a certified weigh station. The weight, called the *tare weight,* is recorded. After your goods are loaded, the truck is weighed again, either at the origin or destination, to determine its *gross weight.* Tare weight is then subtracted from gross weight to yield *net weight*—the weight of your shipment that determines your actual charges. You are entitled to be present at these weighings, and probably should be to prevent what is known in the trade as "bumping up" the weight by loading improperly.

If the actual cost is higher than the estimate, you are required to pay the cost of the estimate plus 10 percent before any goods are unloaded. You have 30 days to pay any remaining money due. For example, if the estimate was $3,000 and the actual charges are $3,500, you would pay only $3,300 (the estimate plus 10 percent) and have 30 days to pay the other $200. Payment must be in cash, money order, bank check, or the like. Personal checks are not normally accepted, so consult your mover. Some companies accept credit cards, but always check with them first. Make sure you understand how payment is to be made so there is no misunderstanding on moving day.

## Binding Estimate

The *binding estimate* is straightforward: The estimator will take inventory and then give you a price.

And that's it. No matter what your shipment weighs, that price is all you are required to pay—it's binding on you and the mover. Indeed, many movers won't even weigh your shipment, because they're bound to the price.

Many movers offer a type of binding estimate called a *best-price estimate.* After the estimate, the van is weighed to determine net weight; then you are offered the lower price.

There is a bewildering array of price plans that you can get, some based only on the line-haul charges and some based on line-haul charges plus other aspects of the move (such as storage). It can get confusing, so our advice is this: Get things explained, take the best price based on an apples-versus-apples comparison, and keep your eye on the bottom line. The discounts are definitely there, no matter how they're presented.

## What's Included

A crucial point, no matter what type of estimate you get, is to make sure you know as much as possible about all charges and all services. In other words, not only should you know about the line-haul charges but also all the extras: the stair carry, elevator carry, additional transportation charge, overtime charge, bulky article charge, third-party service, excessive-distance carry, etc. Always get a written estimate on such charges.

These costs may be easy to determine at the origin point but more difficult to anticipate at the destination. It is advisable to check for obstacles or unusual characteristics at your new residence *before* moving day. This will give you and the mover a more accurate picture of the destination and any difficulties or special circumstances for the unloading. For example, if telephone or cable wires are going to require the truck to park farther from the house than expected, this might result in an excessive-distance carry charge.

## Get a Complete Estimate

Try to find out about all the costs so you can get a complete estimate. In most moves—over 90 percent, according to the ICC—there are few extra charges, but in a worst-case scenario, where you need many extras, the cost of the move could *double*.

Remember that some salespeople may not mention possible extra charges but will give only an estimate on the line-haul charges, storage, and valuation. Once you arrive at your destination and the driver demands payment for those extra services, you're not in a great position to negotiate: All your worldly goods are on the mover's truck. So be sure to ask about *all* possible charges before you hire a mover.

## Binding Estimate Is Best

*Consumer Reports* has found that the binding estimate, or some variation of it, is generally the best deal. It allows you to shop around and get firm prices—something you can't do with nonbinding estimates, because nothing is firm until the net weight is determined.

Not all companies offer binding estimates, but most of the big companies do. It should be one of the questions you ask when you first call a company. Moving companies are allowed to charge for making binding estimates, but most don't.

## Negotiating Estimates

When the estimator comes to your house, a room-by-room survey of your goods will be done, and it is while the estimator is there that you should get an estimate.

That is the time to negotiate discounts as well. Normally, companies will give estimators a range of prices they can charge for a move. Your goal should be to get the lowest price that you can and one that includes all services involved in the move.

You should accompany the estimator as he or she marks down what is to be shipped. A standard form, called the *estimate* or *order for service/estimate*, is used.

## Table of Measurements

At the heart of the estimate is a table of measurements, which lists, room by room, all of the items in a house or apartment and assigns a number of *cubes* to each item. A cube is an industry term that equals 7 pounds. Once the number of cubes is known, the estimator multiplies the number by 7 to determine the approximate weight. The table will also list what is to be shipped—and not shipped—and the cartons used.

## Detailed Estimates

Estimates should be as detailed as possible. You want to know exactly how many cartons will be used, and at what cost; how much that side trip will cost; the cost of the move per 100 pounds of weight, etc. Only when you have it in writing can you be sure that each of the movers is offering the same materials and services. If the estimator simply quotes bottom-line figures, that won't tell you anything about which boxes the mover plans to use, how much they will cost, and how much packing and unpacking charges will be.

Although not a contract, the estimate form is an important document because it is the only written record you have of what is to be moved. Although you will be asked to sign the mover's estimate, it is not a commitment to use that mover. Signing the estimate means only that you have seen it. You should still obtain estimates from other moving companies.

## Addendum Form

Before the move, you can still make changes to the estimate. This is generally done with an addendum form on which changes can be entered to modify the estimate up or down.

For example, a couple of weeks after the estimator visits your house, you discover that you want to move things that were hidden in an attic or storage shed. Or you realize that there are items you don't want to move at all. The addendum form allows you to make these changes. However, changes usually require a return trip

to your home by the estimator. You should allow ample time for the company to do this.

The addendum form may also come into use at the destination if extra services (excessive-distance carry, elevator carry, etc.) are required.

It is important to be as honest as possible with the moving company when you are getting estimates. Being anything less than genuine can lead to unpleasant surprises for both you and the mover.

Many a mover has come into a house on moving day to discover the customer has a few extra things that need to be moved. Those extra things should not turn out to be a room full of furniture.

## Voided Agreements

Extras can void a binding agreement. In fact, some companies have forms for their drivers to fill out should they wish to "challenge" the bid. If the weight in cubes is more than 10 to 15 percent greater than the bid, a challenge is likely. An excessive-weight challenge can affect a binding agreement more than not knowing how many extra services you will need.

## Low-Ball Bids

If you have done your homework in finding a company, it is not likely you will encounter unethical movers, particularly if you are dealing with the larger companies. However, should you get a bid that's significantly lower than the others, even on a binding bid, a scam may be involved.

For example, you may receive four estimates: one for $3,400, another for $3,200, another for $3,350, and one for $1,750. You select the lowest bid. Then, on the day before (or morning of) the move, a contrite official or driver of the company proceeds to tell you that their estimator made a terrible mistake in estimating. Now the move will cost you more money—per-

# Table 2.1 Table of Measurements

NAME OF SHIPPER _____ DATE _____ 19 ____

STREET ADDRESS _____

SHIPPING FROM: _____ TO: _____

| Articles Loaded | Articles Not To Be Shipped | ARTICLE | No. of Pieces | Cube | Total Cube | Articles Loaded | Articles Not To Be Shipped | ARTICLE | No. of Pieces | Cube | Total Cube | Articles Loaded | Articles Not To Be Shipped | ARTICLE | No. of Pieces | Cube | Total Cube |
|---|---|---|---|---|---|---|---|---|---|---|---|---|---|---|---|---|---|
| | | **LIVING ROOM** | | | | | | **BEDROOM** | | | | | | **PORCH/OUTDOOR** | | | |
| | | Bar, Portable | 15 | | | | | Bed Incl Sp/Matt | | | | | | BBQ Grill, Small | | 2 | |
| | | Bench, Frsd/Piano | 5 | | | | | Bed Waterbed Base | 10 | | | | | BBQ Grill, Large | | 10 | |
| | | Bookcase | 20 | | | | | Bed Rollaway | 20 | | | | | Chairs, Aluminum | | 1 | |
| | | Bookshelves, Sect. | 5 | | | | | " Single/Hollywood | 40 | | | | | " Metal | | 3 | |
| | | Cabinet Curio | 10 | | | | | " Std/Dbl. | 60 | | | | | " Wood | | 5 | |
| | | Chair, Straight | 5 | | | | | " Queen | 65 | | | | | Gard. Hose & Tools | | 10 | |
| | | Chair, Arm | 10 | | | | | " King | 70 | | | | | Glider or Settee | | 20 | |
| | | ", Rocker | 12 | | | | | " Bunk (Set 2) | 70 | | | | | Ladder, 6' Step | | 3 | |
| | | ", Occasional | 15 | | | | | Chair, Boudoir | 10 | | | | | Ladder, 8' Metal | | 2 | |
| | | ", Overstuffed | 25 | | | | | Chaise Lounge | 25 | | | | | Ladder, Extension | | 8 | |
| | | Clock, Grandfather | 20 | | | | | Chest, Bachelor | 12 | | | | | Lawn Mower, Hand | | 5 | |
| | | Desk, SM/Winthrop | 22 | | | | | " Cedar | 15 | | | | | Lawn Mower, Power | | 15 | |
| | | Desk, Secretary | 35 | | | | | Chest, Armoire | 30 | | | | | Lawn " Riding (HP) | | 35 | |
| | | Fireplace Equip. | 5 | | | | | Dresser/Vanity Bch | 3 | | | | | Leaf Sweeper | | 5 | |
| | | Footstool | 2 | | | | | Dresser, Vanity | 20 | | | | | Outdoor Child Slide | | 10 | |
| | | Hall Tree Rack | 2 | | | | | Dresser, Single | 30 | | | | | Outdoor Child Gym | | 20 | |
| | | Hall Tree Large | 12 | | | | | Dresser, Double | 40 | | | | | Outdoor Swings | | 30 | |
| | | Lamp, Floor/Pole | 3 | | | | | Dresser, Triple | 50 | | | | | Picnic Table | | 20 | |
| | | Magazine Rack | 2 | | | | | Night Table | 5 | | | | | Picnic Bench | | 15 | |
| | | Music Cabinet | 10 | | | | | Trunk | 5 | | | | | Roller, Lawn | | 15 | |
| | | Piano, Baby Gr/Upr | 70 | | | | | Wardrobe, Small | 20 | | | | | Spreader, Lawn | | 2 | |
| | | Piano, Parlor Gr. | 80 | | | | | Wardrobe, Large | 40 | | | | | Table, Small | | 2 | |
| | | " Spinet/Console | 60 | | | | | | | | | | | Table, Large | | 4 | |
| | | Rugs, Lg. Roll/Pad | 10 | | | | | | | | | | | Umbrella | | 1 | |
| | | Rugs, Sm. Roll/Pad | 3 | | | | | | | | | | | Wheelbarrow | | 8 | |
| | | Sofa, Rattan/Wicker | 10 | | | | | | | | | | | | | | |
| | | Sofa, Sec., Per Sec. | 30 | | | | | | **NURSERY** | | | | | | | | | |
| | | Sofa, Loveseat | 35 | | | | | | Baby Carriage | 4 | | | | | | | | |
| | | Sofa, 3 Cushion | 50 | | | | | | Bathinette | 5 | | | | | | | | |
| | | Sofa, Hide, 4 Cush. | 60 | | | | | | Bed, Youth | 30 | | | | | **OFFICE/ WORK-** | | | |
| | | Tables, Dropl/Occas | 12 | | | | | | Chair, Child's | 3 | | | | | **SHOP/MISC.** | | | |
| | | Tables, Coffee/End | 5 | | | | | | Chest | 12 | | | | | Barbells lbs. | | | |
| | | | | | | | | Chest, Toy | 5 | | | | | Basket (Clothes) | | 5 | |
| | | | | | | | | Crib, Baby | 10 | | | | | Bicycle | | 5 | |
| | | | | | | | | Playpen | 10 | | | | | Tricycle | | 2 | |
| | | | | | | | | Table, Child's | 5 | | | | | Exercycle | | 5 | |
| | | **DINING ROOM** | | | | | | | | | | | | Exercise Machine | | 20 | |
| | | Bench, Harvest | 10 | | | | | | | | | | | Hot Tubs | | | |
| | | Buffet (Base) | 30 | | | | | | | | | | | Bowling Ball/Bag | | 3 | |
| | | Hutch (Top) | 20 | | | | | | **APPLIANCES** | | | | | | Card Table | | 2 | |
| | | Cabinet Corner | 20 | | | | | | Air Cond/Wind Sm. | 15 | | | | | Folding Chairs | | 1 | |
| | | Dining Table | 30 | | | | | | Air Cond/Wind Lg. | 20 | | | | | Clothes Hamper | | 5 | |
| | | " Chair | 5 | | | | | | Dehumidifier | 10 | | | | | Cot, Folding | | 10 | |
| | | Tea Cart | 10 | | | | | | Dishwasher | 20 | | | | | Desk, Office | | 30 | |
| | | | | | | | | Dryer | 25 | | | | | Fan | | 5 | |
| | | | | | | | | Freezer, 10 or less | 30 | | | | | Fern/Plant Stands | | 2 | |
| | | | | | | | | Freezer, 11 to 15 | 45 | | | | | Filing Cab. Crdbd | | 3 | |
| | | **ELECTRONICS** | | | | | | ", 16 or over | 60 | | | | | Filing Cab. 2 drawers | | 10 | |
| | | Entertainment Ctr | 20 | | | | | | Range, 20" Wide | 10 | | | | | Filing Cab. 4 drawers | | 20 | |
| | | PC/Printer | 8 | | | | | | " 30" Wide | 15 | | | | | Footlockers | | 5 | |
| | | Satellite, sm | 15 | | | | | | " 36" Wide | 30 | | | | | Game Table | | 15 | |
| | | Satellite, lg | 25 | | | | | | Refrigerator (CuCp) | | | | | | Golf Bag | | 4 | |
| | | Stereo Component | 8 | | | | | | " 6 cu. ft. or less | 30 | | | | | Heater, Gas/Electric | | 5 | |
| | | Stereo/TV, Console | 15 | | | | | | " 7 to 10 cu. ft. | 45 | | | | | Metal Shelves | | 5 | |
| | | TV, Portable | 5 | | | | | | " 11 cu. ft./over | 60 | | | | | Ping Pong Table | | 40 | |
| | | TV, Table Model | 10 | | | | | | Vacuum Cleaner | 5 | | | | | Pool Table Comp. | | 40 | |
| | | TV, Combination | 25 | | | | | | Washing Machine | 25 | | | | | Pool Table Slate | | 100 | |
| | | TV, Screen | 10 | | | | | | | | | | | | Power Tool Hand Ea | | 3 | |
| | | TV, Stand | 3 | | | | | | | | | | | | Power Tool Stand | | 15 | |
| | | Typewriter, Port. | 5 | | | | | | | | | | | | Sewing Mach., Port. | | 5 | |
| | | VCR | 3 | | | | | | **KITCHEN** | | | | | | " Console | | 10 | |
| | | | | | | | | Bkft. Suite, Chairs | 5 | | | | | " w/Cabinet | | 20 | |
| | | | | | | | | Breakfast Table | 10 | | | | | Sled | | 2 | |
| | | | | | | | | Chair, High | 5 | | | | | Suitcase | | 5 | |
| | | Total Col. 1 | | | | | | Ironing Board | 2 | | | | | Table, Utility | | 5 | |
| | | | | | | | | Kitchen Cabinet | 30 | | | | | Tire | | 3 | |
| | | | | | | | | Microwave Oven | 10 | | | | | Tire w/Rim | | 5 | |
| | | | | | | | | Microwave Std./Tbl. | 10 | | | | | Toolchest, Small | | 5 | |
| | | | | | | | | Serving Cart | 15 | | | | | " Medium | | 10 | |
| | | | | | | | | Stool Bar | 3 | | | | | " Large | | 15 | |
| | | | | | | | | Utility Cabinet | 10 | | | | | Trash Can | | 7 | |
| | | | | | | | | | | | | | | Wagon, Child's | | 5 | |
| | | | | | | | | | | | | | | Work Bench | | 20 | |

| Carton | Carrier Pack | Owner Pack | Tot. Cnt. | Cb. | Tot. Cb. |
|---|---|---|---|---|---|
| Dish-Pack | | | | 10 | |
| | | | | 10 | |
| | | | | 10 | |
| Carton 1.5 | | | | 1.5 | |
| | | | | 1.5 | |
| | | | | 1.5 | |
| Carton 3.0 | | | | 3.0 | |
| | | | | 3.0 | |
| | | | | 3.0 | |
| Carton 4.5 | | | | 4.5 | |
| | | | | 4.5 | |
| | | | | 4.5 | |
| Carton 6.0 | | | | 6.0 | |
| | | | | 6.0 | |
| | | | | 6.0 | |
| Wardrobe | | | | 10 | |
| Crib Matt. | | | | | |
| Single Matt. | | | | | |
| Dbl Matt. | | | | | |
| Qn/Kg Matt. | | | | | |
| Waterbed Matt. | | | | | |
| Mirror Ctn. | | | | | |
| Crates (Dim.) | | | | | |
| | | | | | |
| | | | | | |
| | | | | | |
| | | | | | |
| | | Total | | | |

Total Col. 2

**WEIGHT ADDITIVE**

BOAT   ADDTV WT _____ ACT WT _____
(Less than 14 ft)
BOAT   ADDTV WT _____ ACT WT _____
(More than 14 ft)
BOAT TLR ADDTV WT _____ ACT WT _____
OTHER
        ADDTV WT _____ ACT WT _____

**BULKY ARTICLES**

Automobile (Make, Model)

_____ = _____ lbs.

Other _____ = _____ lbs.

Only the items listed are included in the Total Cost. Any items or additional services added may result in additional cost.

Shipper _____ Date _____

Carrier's Representative _____

| | PCS | CUBE |
|---|---|---|
| Total This Column | | |
| Total Col. 1 | | |
| Total Col. 2 | | |
| Total Cartons | | |
| TOTAL CUBE | | |

Wt. Factor (lbs./cu. ft.) _____

Computed Est. Wt. _____

Total Wt. Additive and
➤ Bulky Art. Wt. _____

**TOTAL EST. WEIGHT** _____

# Table 2.2 Estimate/Order for Service

**Atlas Van Lines** — World-Class Moving
I.C.C.M.C. 79658

**ESTIMATE/ORDER FOR SERVICE**
GENERAL P.O. BOX 509, 1212 ST GEORGE ROAD, EVANSVILLE, IN 47703-0509
OFFICES PHONE 800/252-8885 OUTSIDE IN/AK 812/424-2222 COLLECT INSIDE IN/AK

**Attachment #3**
REGISTRATION NO.

YOUR SHIPMENT IS ☒ STANDARD/ **BLD** ☐ BINDING/ _____

| | | |
|---|---|---|
| SHIPPER **John Brown** | CONSIGNEE **John Brown** | |
| STREET ADDRESS **630 10th Ave.** | STREET ADDRESS **1510 Grace St.** | |
| CITY AND STATE **Evansville, IN** COUNTY **Vanderburgh** | CITY AND STATE **Albuquerque, NM** COUNTY **Bernalillo** | |
| PHONE **(812) 421-6600** | PHONE **(505) 635-1010** | |

## ESTIMATED COST OF CONTAINERS AND PACKING AND UNPACKING SERVICES

| | CONTAINERS ( ) | | | PACKING ( E ) | | | UNPACKING ( G ) | | |
|---|---|---|---|---|---|---|---|---|---|
| | ESTIMATED NUMBER | PER EACH | TOTAL | ESTIMATED NUMBER | PER EACH | TOTAL | ESTIMATED NUMBER | PER EACH | TOTAL |
| DRUM DISH PACK BARREL (OF NOT LESS THAN 5 CU. FT.) | 10 | 15.05 | 150.50 | 10 | 21.60 | 216.00 | 10 | 10.85 | 108.50 |
| LESS THAN 3 CU. FT. | 28 | 3.20 | 89.60 | 28 | 5.50 | 154.00 | | | |
| 3 CU. FT. | 25 | 4.60 | 115.00 | 25 | 8.45 | 211.25 | | | |
| 4.5 CU. FT. | 15 | 5.50 | 82.50 | 15 | 10.35 | 155.25 | | | |
| 6 CU. FT. | 12 | 6.35 | 76.20 | 12 | 11.70 | 140.40 | | | |
| WARDROBE CARTON NOT LESS THAN 10 CU. FT. | 10 | 11.80 | 118.00 | 10 | 6.30 | 63.00 | | | |
| CRIB MATTRESS CNT. | | | | | | | | | |
| MATTRESS CARTON TWIN SIZE (NOT EXCEEDING 39″ x 75″) | | | | | | | | | |
| MATTRESS CARTON REGULAR SIZE (NOT EXCEEDING 54″ x 75″) | | | | | | | | | |
| MATTRESS CARTON KING/QUEEN (EXCEEDING 54″ x 75″) | 6 | 15.95 | 95.70 | 6 | 9.25 | 55.50 | 6 | 4.80 | 28.80 |
| MATTRESS CARTON (39″ x 80″) | | | | | | | | | |
| CORRUGATED MIRROR CARTONS | 8 | 12.15 | 97.20 | 8 | 19.30 | 154.40 | 8 | 9.95 | 79.60 |
| CRATES SHOW TOTAL CU. FT. CHARGEABLE (WHEN CU. FT. RATE APPLIES) | | | | | 10.60 | | | | |
| WHEN MINIMUM CRATES RATES APPLIES | | | | | 42.35 | 42.35 | | 9.25 | 9.25 |
| (12 x 20 x 6) | | | | | | | | | |
| | ESTIMATED CONTAINER | COSTS $ **824.70** | | ESTIMATED PACKING | COSTS $**1192.15** | | ESTIMATED UNPACKING | COSTS $ **226.15** | |

NOTE TO CUSTOMER: Packing containers and materials are your property. The unpacking service includes removal of these items unless you direct otherwise. An additional charge will be assessed for disposal of packing materials from items unpacked by shipper or carrier on a date other than at delivery time.

### VALUATION SELECTION

Unless the shipper expressly releases the shipment to a value of 60 cents per pound per article the maximum liability for loss and damage shall be either the lump sum value declared by the shipper or an amount equal to $1.25 for each pound of rated weight in the shipment whichever is greater. The shipment will move subject to the rules and conditions of the carrier's tariff. Shipper hereby releases the entire shipment to a value not exceeding:

(1) I hereby release this shipment at Atlas legal liability of $.60 per pound per article

_____ (Shipper or Representative)   _____ (Date)

(2) I hereby release this shipment to Atlas with additional carrier's liability at $ _____ (insert amount per pound or lump sum value). The amount inserted must be a minimum of $1.25 per pound times the actual weight

_____ (Shipper or Representative)   _____ (Date)

### FULL VALUE PROTECTION

(3.) By signature below, the shipper elects this protection option excluding the released rate and declared value options (by so doing shipper accepts to the terms of Full Value Protection Plan as provided in carrier's tariffs). Otherwise, the shipment is released as provided in MC-506 elsewhere declared herein.
I declare this shipment to be released with Full Value Protection in the amount of $ **50,000**. This amount must be the sum indicated at the tariff item based on the full value option selected, but not less than $3.50 per lb. times the actual weight of the shipment subject to a $10,000.00 minimum released value per shipment.

FVP DEDUCTIBLE SELECTION
☒ OPTION A  ☐ OPTION B  ☐ OPTION C
NO DEDUCTIBLE  $250 DEDUCTIBLE  $500 DEDUCTIBLE

*John Brown* (signature)
(Shipper or Representative)   (Date)

NOTICE
The shipper signing this contract must insert in one of the spaces above his own signature otherwise the shipment will be deemed released at a maximum value equal to $1.25 times the actual weight of the shipment in pounds.

Extraordinary (Unusual) Value Article Declaration
I acknowledge that I have prepared and retained a copy of the "Inventory of Items Valued in Excess of $100 Per Pound Per Article" that are included in my shipment and that I have given a copy of this Inventory to the carrier's representative. I also acknowledge that the carrier's liability for loss of or damage to any article valued in excess of $100 per pound will be limited to $100 per pound for each pound of such lost or damaged article (based on actual article weight), not to exceed the declared value of the entire shipment, unless I have specifically identified such articles for which a claim for loss or damage is made on the attached inventory.    I decline ☐

Shipper _____ Date _____

CUSTOMER REQUESTED NOTIFICATION OF ACTUAL WEIGHT AND CHARGES ☐ NO  ☒ YES
CUSTOMER'S (SHIPPER'S) CONTACT  ENROUTE ☐  DESTINATION ☐

NAME _____ PHONE _____
STREET _____
CITY & STATE _____

### SPECIAL SERVICE ORDER BY SHIPPER
_____ EXCLUSIVE USE OF VEHICLE _____ CU. FT.
_____ SPACE RESERVATION _____ CU. FT.
_____ LENGTH OF SPACE ORDER _____ FT.
_____ EXPEDITED SERVICE _____ HOISTING OR LOWERING _____ LABOR
_____ EXCESSIVE CARRY _____ STAIRS _____ AUXILIARY SERVICE
_____ PIANO OR ORGAN CARRY _____ ELEVATOR
TRANSIT STORAGE _____ ORIGIN _____ DESTINATION _____ MILES _____
TYPE OF SHIPMENT _____ CHGE. ☐  CREDIT CARD ☐  P.P.D. ☐  C.O.D. ☐

BOOKING AGENT _____ CODE _____
ORIGIN AGENT _____ CODE _____
ADDRESS _____ PHONE _____
CITY & STATE _____
DESTINATION AGENT _____ CODE _____
ADDRESS _____ PHONE _____
CITY & STATE _____

| PACKING DATE REQUESTED | AGREED PICKUP DATE OR PERIOD OF TIME | AGREED DELIVERY DATE OR PERIOD OF TIME |
|---|---|---|
| | | |

ADDITIONAL INSTRUCTIONS OR BILLING INFORMATION
SUBJECT TO MINIMUM OF
WEIGHT _____
CHARGES _____

Shipper hereby makes, constitutes and appoints
(NAME) _____ (ADDRESS) _____ (PHONE) _____
as true and lawful agent for shipper, in shipper's name, place and stead, to give carrier instructions, perform all acts and to execute all documents pertaining to the transportation and service ordered until such time as said transportation and services are performed.

THE CARRIER, BY SIGNATURE OR ITS REPRESENTATIVE, HEREBY ACCEPTS THIS ORDER FOR SERVICES AND AGREES TO PERFORM THE SERVICES OUTLINED HEREIN.

### SERVICE CHARGES

| | | |
|---|---|---|
| Tariff No. **400-H** Miles **1202** | | SERVICE CHARGES |
| **8,000** lb. Base Trans. Charge $ **5,264.00** | | |
| 1. **1,500** lbs @ **54.60** /cwt. $ **819.00** | | **6,083.00** |
| 2. Insurance Surcharge **Item 60 (4%)** | | **243.32** |
| 3. Add'l Trans. (surcharge) ☒ Orig. **.42** ☒ Dest. **.42** | | **79.80** |
| 4. Extra Pickups or Deliveries No. _____ | | |
| 5. Excessive Carry - Total **150** Less 75 **2 = 2.50** | | **237.50** |
| 6. Elevators Orig. _____ Dest. _____ | | |
| 7. Stair Carry - Orig. No. Flights _____ Dest No. Flights _____ | | |
| 8. Piano Handling Out _____ In _____ Hoist _____ | | |
| 9. Appliance Services _____ To _____ | | |
| 10. Bulky Articles _____ | | |
| 11. Other Services _____ | | |
| 12. _____ | | |
| 13. Total Lines 1 thru 12 | | **6,643.62** |
| 14. Valuation (See Valuation Selection) **50,000-A** | | **350.00** |
| 15. Third Party Service _____ | | |
| 16. SIT Valuation Charge _____ | | |
| Transit Storage From _____ | | |
| 17. _____ lbs @ _____ cwt. first day | | |
| 18. cwt. ea. add'l. day _____ | | |
| 19. Warehouse Handling _____ | | |
| 20. Cartage To Whse. _____ Mi. _____ | | |
| 21. Total Lines 16 thru 20 _____ | | |

### ESTIMATE SUMMARY

| | | |
|---|---|---|
| COST OF CONTAINERS | **824.70** a | ☐ TOTAL BINDING CHARGES (See Note 1) $ _____ |
| COST OF PACKING | **1,192.15** b | |
| COST OF UNPACKING | **226.15** c | |
| TOTAL LINE 13 | **6,643.62** d | ESTIMATE VALID THROUGH _ / _ / _ |
| SUBTOTAL LINES a THRU d | **8,886.62** e | ☒ TOTAL ESTIMATE CHARGES (See Note 2 and 3) $ **6,126.30** |
| **BLD 135** | (**3,110.32**) f | |
| VALUATION CHGS. LINE 14 | **350.00** g | ☒ 110% COLLECT OPTION $ **6,738.93** |
| TOTAL LINES 15 & 21 | | h |
| TOTAL LINES e THRU h | **6,126.30** i | |

1. In the event additional services are required and provided, the cost of these will be in addition to the amount stated above. Such services and applicable charges will be based upon the Tariff rates in effect on the date of this estimate.

2. NOTE: These charges cover only the articles and services listed. It is not a guarantee that the actual charges will not exceed the amount of the estimate. When estimates are provided at the request of shipper, common carriers are required by law to collect transportation and other incidental charges on the basis of the rates shown in their lawfully published tariffs regardless of prior rate quotations made by the carrier or its agents. Exact charges for loading, transporting and unloading are based upon the weight or volume of the goods transported and such charges may not be determined prior to the time the goods are loaded on the van. Charges for additional services will be added to the transportation charges.

3. If the total tariff charges for the listed services exceed the estimate (2) by more than ten percent then upon your request the carrier must relinquish possession of your shipment upon payment in advance of the total estimated tariff charges shown on the bill of lading of freight bill plus ten percent. You are still obligated to pay the balance of the total charges within 30 days. If the shipper elects this option, he must pay upon delivery the amount of the estimated charges plus ten percent in cash, cashier check, or postal money order.

CARRIER'S REPRESENTATIVE _____ AGENT CODE _____

1. In accordance with Rules and Regulations of the Interstate Commerce Commission, I have received a copy of Publication OCP - 100 "Your Rights and Responsibilities When You Move," Summary of Carrier's Dispute Settlement Program, the carrier's most recent Annual Performance Report, and a written description of the carrier's customer complaint and inquiry procedure.

2. I have been advised of my rights to observe the weighing of my shipment and informed of the location of scale to be used. I do ☐ do not ☐ desire to observe the weighing. (Non-binding).

3. I hereby acknowledge receipt of a copy of this order for service received identified herein.

4. All charges to be paid in cash, postal money order or cashier's check payable to Atlas Van Lines.

BY X _____ X _____
Atlas Agent    Code No.    Representative    Shipper or his agent

**ATLAS REVENUE ACCOUNTING**
D.C.-203018 Rev. 1/91

# Table 2.3 Amendment to Order for Service

General Offices:
P.O. Box 509, 1212 St. George Road,
Evansville, Indiana 47703
Phone 812-424-2222
800-252-8885

REGISTRATION NO.

## AMENDMENT TO ORDER FOR SERVICE

Name of
Shipper _____

Date of this
Amendment _____

Origin_____ Destination_____
CITY AND STATE                                    CITY AND STATE

SHIPPER AGREES TO AMEND THE ORDER FOR SERVICE AND ASSENTS TO A REVISED ESTIMATE OF CHARGES (IF ANY) TO PROVIDE FOR THE FOLLOWING DESCRIBED CHANGES. ALL OTHER PROVISIONS OF THE ORDER FOR SERVICE AND ESTIMATE OF CHARGES ARE INCORPORATED HEREIN BY REFERENCE.

TO CHANGE THE LOADING AND DELIVERY TO THE FOLLOWING:

LOAD ON                                           DELIVER

_____          during_____
SPECIFIC DATE                                             PERIOD OF TIME (DATES INCLUSIVE)

OR                                                OR

Load during_____   on _____
PERIOD OF TIME (DATES INCLUSIVE)                          SPECIFIC DATE

TO CHANGE THE DESTINATION TO THE FOLLOWING:

_____

| TO PROVIDE THE FOLLOWING ADDITIONAL SERVICES: (MAY INCLUDE PACKING CHARGES, ADDITIONAL ITEMS IN SHIPMENT, STORAGE - IN - TRANSIT, AND DESTINATION SERVICES.) | ESTIMATED CHARGES |
|---|---|
| | |
| | |
| | |
| | |
| | |
| | |

ORIGINAL
Estimated Charges     $ _____

ADDITIONAL
Estimated Charges     $ _____

NEW TOTAL
Estimated Charges     $ _____

TOTAL AMOUNT TO BE REQUIRED TO
BE PAID IN CASH, CERTIFIED CHECK,
TRAVELER'S CHECK, OR BANK CHECK
ON DAY OF DELIVERY.

(110% of New Total
Estimated Charges)     $ _____

BALANCE DUE 30 DAYS AFTER DELIVERY
EXCLUSIVE OF SATURDAYS, SUNDAYS & HOLIDAYS.

Additional Estimated Charges  $ _____

THE ABOVE CHANGES WERE REQUESTED AND APPROVED
BY THE SHIPPER OR THE SHIPPER'S REPRESENTATIVE.

_____
SHIPPER OR HIS REPRESENTATIVE

## ATLAS VAN LINES, INC.

By _____
AGENT OR DRIVER          CODE NO.

ATLAS COPY

DC 201004

haps in line with the other bids, or even higher. These scams exploit the difficulty of having to get another mover so close to moving day.

As a hedge against such a dilemma, question the company about a comparatively lower price and call a couple of weeks before the move to confirm the figures and details.

## IMPORTANT POINTS

• Mover-supplied cartons and packing services add to the cost of a move—they're rarely free.

• Extra services—for example, an excessive-distance carry or elevator carry—can also add to the cost of a move.

• Valuation is not the same thing as insurance. With valuation, you must prove the carrier's liability.

• Most professionals say that a binding estimate is the best type to get.

• Obtain a complete estimate, one based not only on line-haul charges but also on extra service charges, storage fees, and valuation costs.

# 3

# Packing

THERE are three ways to pack for a move: the movers pack everything, you pack everything yourself, or you and the movers share the packing.

If the mover does it all, the usual procedure is for the company to send a couple of packers to your home a day or so before the move (that's enough time for experienced packers), and they perform the job. But professional packers are costly. It is estimated that having professionals do the packing can easily double moving costs because you will be charged not only for the packing but also for the boxes, and these are expensive.

The second option, doing it all yourself, may not be that difficult, although it will involve extra time and effort. You can purchase boxes, but there are a wide variety of free sources for them.

Overall, the best approach may be for you to do some of the work and to let the professionals do the rest. For instance, you could pack the items that involve little or no risk of damage and let the movers take it from there. Of course, it's going to take some extra time to do your share of the packing, so if you have a household full of goods to move, plan to do it over a couple of weeks.

## WHO SHOULD PACK WHAT

You should pack compact objects such as small appliances, books, clothing, silverware, tools, cutlery, and linens—things with virtually no breakable parts. It is best to have the movers pack such delicate items as china, mirrors, glassware, certain electronic equipment, etc.—anything very fragile. By scrutinizing your belongings in advance, you can reach a more informed decision on what you will pack and what would be best for the mover to pack.

# CARTONS

Successful do-it-yourself packing starts with boxes. A variety of sizes will be required, as well as some specialized cartons. You can buy all your boxes from the mover, but this is expensive (see box that follows). A less costly way to get boxes, although still not cheap, is to buy them from a truck rental company.

Of course, the very best way is to get them for free. You may need a couple of months to accumulate what you need, but there are several good sources for empty boxes.

First, use the following guide to obtain the correct size and to plan which items to store in each box. Try to get boxes as close to the sizes listed as possible, because they've been found to work best. For example, you can use bigger boxes for books, but the box can end up so heavy that it will be difficult to lift. Or it may be classified as overweight (see chapter 4) if you decide to ship it separately.

• *Book carton.* This box—13 inches by 13 inches by 16 inches—is the size commonly used to ship books. It is also excellent for other small, heavy objects such as appliances, tools, canned goods, and records (records placed on their edges will fit perfectly).

• *Medium box.* This box—18 inches by 18 inches by 16 inches—can hold double what the book carton can. It is good for packing an assortment of items that are not particularly heavy, such as pots and pans, garden equipment, light hand/power tools, nonperishable food items (macaroni, rice, cereal), and other miscellaneous objects.

• *Large box.* This box—18 inches by 18 inches by 24 inches—is best for large, light items such as lamp shades, linens, pillows, stuffed toys, etc. (items with size or bulk but relatively little weight).

## Specialized Boxes

In addition to the aforementioned cartons, there are a number of specialized ones that can be purchased.

• *Mattress carton.* These come in different dimensions to fit all mattress sizes. You can pack a mattress without a box, but a box protects the mattress against inclement weather, makes it easier to load, and prevents the fabric cover from being snagged.

• *Dish pack.* This box is 18 inches by 18 inches by 30 inches, with cardboard that is twice as thick as on standard boxes. The interior may have various cardboard dividers. Dish packs are designed for shipping such fragile items as china, glassware, lamp bases, statuary, and anything else that is susceptible to being damaged easily.

• *Mirror carton.* This box telescopes (one box fits snugly into another) to provide better protection for a mirror or other glass slabs.

• *Wardrobe carton.* This box—21 inches by 24 inches by 48 inches—contains a two-foot metal bar going across the top for hanging garments. This means you can take your clothes out of your closets and hang them directly in the box. You can save money on professional iron-

---

## Buying Boxes

The most expensive way to buy boxes is in new condition from a moving company. However, there are a couple of cheaper alternatives.

One is to buy *used* boxes from the moving company. Prices will vary from company to company, but you can save at least 75 percent of the cost.

Buying from do-it-yourself truck rental companies is another option, and they charge much less than a mover does—generally, one-fourth to one-third the price of a mover's boxes before discounts. Also, truck rental companies charge different prices, so a survey of three or four companies may result in solid savings.

ing and dry-cleaning bills with this carton and also save the time and effort required to fold and pack clothing. Furthermore, the box can be used for hanging plants and curtains or draperies—anything that can be hung and would otherwise pose difficulties in packing. Wardrobe cartons are also good for long objects such as hunting rifles, fishing rods, or something similarly shaped.

• *Specially constructed boxes.* If need be, you can also construct, or have constructed, wooden boxes for extra-fragile or difficult-to-ship items. The moving company may do it for you, or you can ask someone who specializes in shipping goods.

## Free Boxes

Stores are a good source of free boxes. Before starting to collect the boxes, however, have a conversation with store personnel to alert them to your needs. Tipping doesn't hurt either (someone may have to disrupt his or her routine to accommodate you).

Look for sturdy cardboard boxes. Since wine and liquor bottles are heavy, the boxes they come in are excellent for moving. But make sure you tell store personnel to leave the tops on.

*Tip:* Boxes without tops are useless in mov-

ing. Also, check your boxes for insects before making your selection.

One possible source for free boxes is any supermarket, but you have to determine their quality. Some supermarket boxes are made of flimsy cardboard that can easily collapse; others, such as ones that hold large juice containers, may be quite strong. Supermarkets usually have larger-size boxes than do liquor stores.

## Other Sources

Don't overlook specialized stores either, such as office supply establishments, computer supply outlets, or bookstores. You might even check the telephone book for companies that sell boxes. But assuming the company will sell retail, don't expect to save a lot of money unless you're buying in mass quantities.

You can also buy boxes from do-it-yourself truck rental companies. In some cases, sizes vary slightly from the ones previously described, but they are close enough to serve the same purpose.

Another possible source is moving companies themselves. Boxes can be had for free or at cut-rate prices. Movers usually have used, unwanted boxes, so it pays to inquire.

---

### How Many Boxes?

To determine how many boxes you will need, use the following guidelines:

*For one or two rooms:* 7 small, 3 medium, 3 large, 1 dish pack, and 2 wardrobe boxes.

*For three to four rooms:* 15 small, 8 medium, 6 large, 2 dish packs, and 4 wardrobe boxes.

*For five to six rooms:* 20 small, 12 medium, 8 large, 3 dish packs, and 6 wardrobe boxes.

*For seven to eight rooms:* 30 small, 20 medium, 12 large, 4 dish packs, and 8 wardrobe boxes.

---

## OTHER PACKING SUPPLIES

Another packing supply needed for a move is newspaper. When crumpled and packed into boxes, it makes an excellent shock absorber. In fact, moving companies use newsprint extensively for packing. The only difference between their paper (called "white paper") and regular newsprint is that it has no printing on it. Movers know that ink comes off newsprint and smudges or mars some items.

One way to prevent smudging is to shield susceptible items from the newsprint ink by storing them in plastic bags. Hence, a variety of plastic bags, from sandwich size up to 30-gallon size (for something like a lamp shade), should be purchased. Such bags can also be used in other ways, including storing loose parts or hardware. (Remember to label bags and tape them to larger items.)

### Use Newspaper Selectively

Another option is to use newspaper only with certain items and then simply wash the items later, if necessary. But you have to be careful what you wrap in newspaper. For example, newsprint ink can get embedded in fine china and be very difficult to remove.

Our suggestion is to buy white paper, as previously described, and avoid the hassle of protecting items against ink smudges. It is sold by the pound, so just check your telephone book and call around to get the best buy. Tissue paper is a good choice for wrapping fragile items because it fits snugly into grooves and fretwork for better protection.

Plastic ties also come in handy, and tape is essential for packing. Wide, clear, adhesive-backed tape—commonly called packaging tape—works very well. A ball of sisal twine will also be useful.

## SPECIALIZED MATERIALS

There are also a variety of specialized materials that are available, including bubble wrap, plastic peanuts (or popcorn), and more. You might take a look at what's available from the movers—van lines as well as do-it-yourself movers—and packaging stores to see who has the best price. Such carton stuffers might be just what you need for specialized items.

## MARK BOXES

Contents of all boxes should be marked. Using felt-tip marking pens, write on the sides or faces of boxes rather than just the tops, so they can be read when stacked. If you mark only the tops, you will have to lift and turn each stacked box to read the contents.

Some movers will supply you with free box labels and stickers, so ask if they are available and use them. You can also purchase them from movers.

You can use scissors for cutting tape or rope, but a lightweight razor knife or utility knife will generally work quicker and better.

## CENTRAL PACKING PLACE

As things are brought out to be packed, disarray tends to occur in a house. You should establish a central place for packing and wrapping, away from the clutter. A kitchen table works well, but you might set up two or three areas—satellite stations—to save steps. Card tables or the like serve this purpose well. It is a good idea to cover the tables with a mattress cover, blanket, or something similarly soft to protect them from chipping against a hard surface. If a table is not available, you can stack some sturdy boxes and then lay a sheet of plywood over them.

*Tip:* When wrapping an item, it's best to lay it on a stack of paper in the center of the table, then roll the item over the paper to wrap it.

## GENERAL PACKING TIPS

When packing, it's good to keep the following things in mind:

• Pack one room at a time, marking boxes with the name of each room. Try not to pack items from different rooms in the same box.

• Don't overload cartons. Limit each to under 30 pounds. Boxes heavier than this will be difficult to lift.

• Pack delicate items individually.

• Pack so that items are well cushioned with blank newsprint or tissue paper.

• Pack things so they won't move inside boxes.

• Pack items that are similar together; for example, don't pack delicate things with heavy items.

• Keep small parts, such as knobs or screws, together with the objects they came from.

• When packing items of various weights in a box, place the heaviest things at the bottom, the next heaviest in the middle, and the lightest items on top.

• If you have a floor plan of your new home, mark boxes with specific colors that correspond to colors used in that plan—for example, yellow for the master bedroom, green for the kitchen, etc.

# PACKING LARGE APPLIANCES

Before packing large appliances, be sure they are clean and dry and don't contain water, grease, or soil that will lead to mildew and other problems (particularly if the items stay in storage for a while). Many large appliances must also be "serviced," or prepared for shipment. If you have any questions, refer to your owner's manual (assuming you have one) or contact the manufacturer directly. (Call 800-555-1212 to see if your manufacturer has a toll-free number where you can get technical assistance.)

Large appliances themselves can be used as storage units (you can store such things as blankets and linens inside them). Appliance cords can be coiled with twist ties, then taped to the backs of the appliances.

## Washer

Disconnect and drain the hoses, and thoroughly wipe dry any interior surfaces that are wet. Open the lid or door and air out prior to taping the door securely shut. Clean the tub and lint fil-

ter with a soft, dry cloth. Also, block the motor so it won't move. This can be done with cardboard and rags, or you can purchase a specialized Styrofoam block. Sometimes you can tighten parts beneath the machine (check your owner's manual).

If you are moving a washer during cold weather, some manufacturers suggest pouring a quart of antifreeze in the tub to keep any remaining water from freezing and damaging the machine. If this is done, run the machine an entire cycle at your destination before using it for regular washes.

## Refrigerator

Defrost the appliance a few days before the move. Also, drain any water from the ice maker, and empty the pan under the refrigerator. Wipe dry.

To prevent damage to shelves inside the refrigerator, remove, clean, and pack them separately in a box, cushioning them from each other with wadded-up newspaper.

Then, clean the inside of the refrigerator, drying it completely. In addition, clean the back, vacuuming the compressor area for dust.

It's a good idea to double-check your work. No other large appliance is more susceptible to collecting mildew and bad odors than a refrigerator.

*Tip:* To guard against mildew, place a sock containing ground coffee or a barbecue charcoal inside the refrigerator, or use a commercially available product.

## Range

Disconnect gas lines (make sure gas is shut off first) or electric lines. Utility companies will be able to furnish you with advice on how to do this, or they may do it for you.

Next, take off removable parts and wash in warm, soapy water as allowed by the manufacturer. (Don't wash the plug or electric coils.) Place dry parts inside the machine, properly blocked so they won't move around. Clean the range and tape the cord to the back.

## Taking Your Major Appliances

Should you take your major appliances with you when you move? In some cases it pays to take your appliances, but only if they are in good condition. In addition, your new home may not be equipped with all the appliances you need. But you should consider the cost of moving your large appliances before you decide to take them with you.

You may have no choice but to leave them if they are expected to be included in the sale of your house. Items like dishwashers, ovens and ranges, through-the-wall air conditioners, built-in refrigerators, and built-in microwave ovens are usually included in the contract. Your intentions about under-the-counter appliances should be carefully specified. There can be a good deal of misunderstanding about whether or not these items are part of the bargain.

Remember to compare your present large appliances with your needs in your new home. For instance, if you have double-hung windows and are moving to a location with sliding windows (or vice versa), any window-mounted room air conditioners you now own may be useless in your new location.

Also, moving refrigerators with automatic ice makers or through-the-door ice and water dispensers may be problematic. If you have such a refrigerator, you may have to go through the trouble of tapping into a water line in your new residence. Be aware that if you are moving into a house where the owner is providing you with a refrigerator with ice-making capabilities, you may be receiving a headache. *Consumer Reports* data show that the odds you'll have trouble almost double with a through-the-door ice and water dispenser refrigerator, compared to a refrigerator without these capabilities.

### Dishwasher

Disconnect the electric and water connections, and drain the hoses as needed (either into a sink or in a pan); then dry the interior thoroughly. (Leave the lid or door open for a few days.) Place the dry hoses inside the washer, first wrapping them with paper or towels.

### Dryer

Clean the exterior with an appliance cleaner and a soft, damp cloth. Use a dry paper towel or your fingers to remove debris from the lint screen. Use a damp sponge (make sure the appliance is turned off) to remove inside dust. Remove discoloration from the dryer drum with a mild liquid detergent. In addition, disengage the exhaust system.

Finally, load some old rags in the dryer and run it awhile to remove residual soap scum; then dry the drum. Coil and tape the cord to the dryer's body.

## DISHES

The best strategy for packing dishes is to pack them individually, with the heaviest dishes on the bottom, the next heaviest on top of these, and so forth. Typically, you would place platters on the bottom, dinner plates next, and small dishes on top of them.

To wrap dishes, first place one dish on top of the wrapping paper and fold the edges in. Then, nest another plate on top of this, fold more paper inward, and repeat for one or two more plates, wrapping the entire bundle.

*Tip:* To prevent cracking, place dishes on their edges (never flat) in the box.

## SMALL APPLIANCES

Such items as blenders, toasters, can openers, and other small appliances should be packed individually or together in small boxes. First, though, coil the cords, tie them with tie wraps, and tape them to the appliances. Wrap each appliance in paper and/or place in a plastic bag, then wrap in a cushion of paper; put more paper in the box.

# FURNITURE

Furniture comes in a variety of sizes and shapes. The following is a description of common furniture pieces and how you might prepare them for moving.

## Small Tables

Night tables, coffee tables, and the like can be used as miniature storage containers themselves.

First, remove fragile items—such as glass bottles that could rattle around and break—from inside table drawers. Fill the drawers with soft, light items, such as linens, and tape or tie compartments closed so they won't open during the trip.

Cover the table with a blanket, or otherwise protect it with bubble wrap or similar protection.

## Lamps

First, remove the shade by unscrewing the decorative nut at the top of the lamp. Remove the bulb, then the harp (the bow-shaped wire that supports the shade) at the base by lifting up. Wrap a generous amount of paper around the base and tape in place. Store the base in a tall box, first filling it with wadded-up newspaper so it won't move. Close and tape the box securely. More than one base can be put in a box, but wrap each one individually.

For a floor-mount type of lamp, proceed as above, but try to unscrew the post from the base, coiling the cord tightly around the post.

## Shades

Pack shades in well-cushioned boxes (use wrapping paper). A shade can also be wrapped in a plastic bag. A number of smaller shades can be nested inside one another, but wrap them individually before nesting them.

When handling any shade, touch the wire portion rather than the fabric to avoid the possibility of soiling it.

## Dressers

These can be left intact. You can also use drawer space to pack lighter items, but not so many that the dresser becomes overly difficult to lift.

If the dresser has casters, it's a good idea to take these off (just pull them out) so the dresser can't roll. Drop the casters in a plastic bag, and tape the bag inside a drawer.

Take off any protruding hardware items (like handles), or cover them with taped-on paper so they don't scratch other items.

## Desks

If your desk has many items in the drawers, such as paper clips, erasers, and other stationery supplies, these should be packed separately in a box. If it contains larger items, pack the drawers with linens or wadded-up paper to keep these items from moving around.

## File Cabinets

Some file cabinets' drawers have sliding metal partitions, which should be pulled forward and locked in place so the drawer contents won't move around too much.

## Pictures and Mirrors

If the pictures are small, wrap them individually and stack them on edge, side by side in a box. If they are large, they should be packed individually in glass packs or mirror cartons. Wrap them with paper first, then stuff the box with more paper to minimize movement. If you wish, you can also build your own glass packs or mirror boxes with cardboard and tape.

Mirrors may be packed as described here, but to help prevent damage to larger ones, adhere masking tape in crisscross patterns on the glass.

### Beds

Disassemble bed parts (frame, headboard, etc.), and label where each part goes. Tape slats and the like together. For the mattress (and the box spring), a mattress box is a good investment. To keep the mattress from getting soiled, leave the slipcovers on. (For information on moving water beds, see page 38.)

### Small Items

Small items are easier for the movers to manage if they are packed in a box, so keep that in mind when thinking about how to prepare small shelves, corner shelves, and other odd-shaped items for moving. Put them in a box, protecting them with newspaper, if necessary.

## CLOTHES

Clothes can be weighty, so you may want to donate or sell whatever you can before you move. If you are packing up suits and other items that can be hung straight up, it may pay to purchase wardrobe cartons. To facilitate unloading, all the hangers should face the same direction. When loaded, wardrobe cartons can weigh 70 to 100 pounds.

Clothing in dressers may be left as is, but extra items that might overload drawers should not be added; the excess weight can damage the dresser. Most clothing can also be packed in medium-size boxes.

Clothes can be moved in a clothes hamper. You can tape it shut with easy-release masking tape, the kind normally used by painters. This will keep the hamper closed without damaging the finish. Ordinary masking tape can bruise or scrape when you pull it off.

## ELECTRONIC EQUIPMENT

• *Televisions.* A TV normally doesn't need to be boxed. The movers will simply wrap a blanket around it. First, though, pull off any knobs and pack them in a plastic bag so they don't get clipped off during the move.

A portable television, however, is best shipped in a box. It should be stored right side up and the box labeled that way.

• *Microwave ovens.* Pack in the original box, then wrap a moving blanket around it.

• *Stereos.* Obviously, it's important to pack this kind of equipment so that any movement is minimized. Use boxes that this equipment can fit into snugly (the original boxes are best), buttressing with wadded-up newspaper as needed. If the arm of a turntable has a locking device, tape it and other potentially movable parts securely. Also, unplug wires and wrap them with tape, labeling them so you can easily replug them in their original positions later.

Affix "Fragile" labels to these boxes, noting with an arrow which side is up.

## SATELLITE DISH

Before deciding to ship a satellite dish, make sure it will work in your new location. A satellite dish dealer or installer can determine this. (You should also check with local authorities to see if you will even be allowed to install one.) Interference from telephone wires and microwaves should also be considered.

Unless you know exactly how to pack a satellite dish, it should be packed by a specialist.

# Moving a Boat

Ironically, the trip a boat makes on a highway can be a rougher experience than a journey on the high seas. Therefore, how you transport it should be carefully considered.

A moving company will move your boat so long as it can fit in the van, but if you are a little wary of this prospect, or the boat is too big, you can hire a company that specializes in moving boats. Some transport only regionally, but others will go anywhere.

You can start your search by looking through the telephone book, or you can inquire at a boatyard. If you know someone who has had a boat moved, you can ask him or her for the name of a reliable mover.

If you hire a boat mover, you can normally get insurance up to $100,000 (and more if your boat is worth more). Just have a rider added to your marine policy. A caveat here is that most movers, if not all, will demand that they use their cradle for transporting the boat (and thus charge you for this service). Your own cradle may be perfectly adequate for supporting your boat in a boatyard, but it may not be able to withstand a 1,000-mile trip.

Interstate moves of a boat are regulated by the ICC. Intrastate moves may or may not be, depending on the state.

As with household moves, the order of the day is to check prices. Call three or four companies to get bids, and find out exactly what they will provide. The first 100 miles are the most expensive in moving a boat. The more mileage, the lower the rate. Generally, expect to pay $1.50 per mile. For example, to ship a 30-foot boat that is 10 feet 6 inches wide from Indianapolis to Baltimore would cost approximately $1,500; from Chicago to Los Angeles, around $2,800. (Included in these prices are the costs of permits, which vary from state to state. In some states, if the boat is beyond a certain size, there will be extra permit charges.)

## Preparing the Boat

To get your boat ready for the trip, begin by draining all the tanks, particularly the gas tank; then tape drawers closed with safe-release masking tape. Disconnect the battery and take out electronic equipment that is not locked into bulkheads, including radios housed in metal frames. Wrap such equipment in bubble wrap or a similarly soft material, and store it in lockers. Tape cardboard over dials to guard faces.

Just as you would for a household move, remove anything that's loose or hanging from the boat. You don't want something hurtling around the cabin.

To prepare the exterior of the boat, remove lifelines and any netting (diesel fumes from the truck can stain lifelines). You can cover trim and the hull with plastic or canvas, but it must be secure or it can come loose and mar the finish of your boat.

For a sailboat, remove the rudder and tie it down on the trailer. In addition, the mast should be unstepped. When doing this, the wires that secure the mast should be carefully labeled to avoid confusion later when remounting it. Wires should be tied off so they don't work their way up the mast and vanish during transport.

Don't forget to remove rigging. If halyards are internal, leave a guideline to ease rerunning later. Coil and label each one. Coil standard rigging, too, labeling each with tape. Protect turnbuckles by removing and stowing them, or wrap each in a sock, lashing it into place. Take off spreaders, antennas, wind vanes, and masthead lights; you can leave mast-mounted winches on.

If your boat is too tall to pass under certain obstacles (such as bridges), you can reduce its height by removing any of a variety of things, including ventilation cowling, window screens, and cabin-top winches. This can conceivably reduce boat height three to four inches.

## Inspection

Just as with your household goods, the mover will inspect your boat for damage prior to transport and note comments on an inventory sheet. This will be entered on the bill of lading, which you will be required to sign. A crane will then be used to lift the boat into position on the cradle. Make sure the movers have secured it tightly and that cradle sag is minimized.

At your destination, inspect the boat and note any damage. As with household goods, it's a good idea to take pictures, before and after, to help prove a claim. At this point, you should clean the boat and perform any needed maintenance chores.

There are three kinds of dishes, and each requires a different packing method.

*Solid dishes* are difficult to ship. If the dish is more than 8 feet in diameter, a crate must be built for it and it must be shipped in a separate vehicle. If less than 8 feet, the dish can go in the van but must be crated.

*Mesh dishes* are easy to move because they can be taken apart and the pieces carefully packed.

*Paneled dishes* have four to six panels and can also be taken apart simply and packed like household goods.

## MISCELLANEOUS

• *Toys.* A large box is good for toys; a clean plastic garbage can may also be used.

• *Sewing machines.* With a cabinet-style sewing machine, unscrew it from the cabinet. Pack it in a box, first stripping the unit of bobbins and accessories (place them in a plastic bag inside the box with the unit). The cabinet itself can be protected by wrapping it with a mover's blanket.

With a portable sewing machine, pack it in a sturdy box to reduce movement. If it has a carrying case, ship it as is.

• *Water beds.* The first step in moving a water bed is to drain the mattress. How this is done depends on the type of bed. If you're not sure, contact the manufacturer, but here are three ways: (1) You can do it fairly rapidly—under a half hour—with an electric pump (you can rent one), (2) you can use a drain pump and faucet adapter, or (3) you can siphon the water out. The last two ways will take longer than the first.

After draining the mattress, disassemble the bed. As you remove the braces, screws, and other small parts, drop them into a plastic bag and tape the bag to the bed frame. As with other items subject to getting scratched, wrap the frame in pads.

A water bed mattress, of course, is not like an ordinary one. It can be folded, but care must be taken so as not to damage baffles inside. First, fold the mattress in thirds, either folding the ends in toward the middle or the side, then fold it in half. Pack it in a carton with blankets.

Roll the heating pad up carefully, so as not to damage the wires inside. If you expect the mattress to be stored more than five weeks, add a mildew inhibitor.

• *Hot tubs.* For moving a hot tub, a mover will impose a "bulky article" charge. If you think that it may be difficult to maintain the hot tub at your new home (depending on whether you have a service contract and the warrantor's location), you may not want to move it at all.

The heart of a hot tub is the heater and related equipment. On some models, it's best to take the heater off—it's normally bolted in place—then drain, disassemble, and ship it in a separate sturdy box. Some manufacturers suggest leaving heating units in place.

The tub should be emptied before moving day. This can usually be done by securing a hose to the threaded drain on the unit.

If the tub will be transported during cold weather, first drain the plumbing system, blowing the water out with a high-pressure vacuum. Standing water can turn to ice, expand, and rupture pipes. If you're not sure exactly how to drain the system, have the dealer do it for you.

Once the hot tub has been relocated, the moving company normally will not reassemble the unit. You will have to arrange for this, or have the destination agent do so.

• *Wine collections.* The main concern when moving a wine collection is temperature. Most good wine should be moved when the temperature is about 55°F. Hence, the best time to move is in the spring or late fall, when temperatures are generally around this mark. Temperature is not so critical with less expensive wines.

Moving the collection by car may be effective, because you can control the car's temperature, but if the wine is being transported in the summer or winter months, you might want to ship it via air.

Wine that is to be moved should, of course, be carefully packed. A good way to pack wine, assuming you're shipping it yourself, is to use wine boxes from the liquor store.

# WHAT TO KEEP, WHAT TO LEAVE BEHIND

Before you move, it's an excellent idea to dispose of, sell, or donate things you don't need. Doing this can make the move easier and less expensive. But deciding what to keep can sometimes be difficult.

## Volatile Materials

It's against the law to transport propane tanks, gasoline, and other flammable products such as naphtha, acetone, lacquer thinner, paint thinners (mineral spirits), and denatured alcohol, which are simply too dangerous to ship and should not be taken with you. Moreover, movers can and will refuse to ship such materials.

If the materials are in portable containers (cans or plastic jugs), you can try giving them away. Perhaps you have a relative with a gas-powered lawn mower who could use a gallon or two of fuel. Or you may have a friend who is a handyperson and could make good use of your mineral spirits or turpentine. If you know a boater, ask if he or she can use that gallon of acetone you keep for boat repairs.

You may also be able to sell these materials at a garage sale. If not, call your local Environmental Protection Agency (EPA) office to find out how best to dispose of them.

## Plants

It's easy to get attached to trees or plants inside or outside your home, but there are a number of reasons for not moving them. In some cases, they simply may not survive the move. When you uproot a tree or plant, you are in effect ripping it away from its life-support system. This can be traumatic, no matter how much loving care you administer in the process.

It is easier to move an indoor plant—or any plant that is potted—but there is no guarantee that it will survive the process either. Another consideration is that the new environment may not be as hospitable for the plant as the old one was. The temperature may be too hot or too cold, the lighting may not be the same, or the humidity too high or too low.

***Is Your Plant Legal?*** Additionally, a number of states ban the importation of certain kinds of plants, not because they oppose the plants themselves but because of the possibility of their harboring unwanted insects, such as the gypsy moth. In some states, there is a ban against all imported plants; in other states, you must first get a certificate of health for the plant from your home state.

***Space Considerations.*** One other argument against moving plants or trees is that it may be physically too difficult, or there may not be enough room for them. It may be better to leave the old apple tree where it is.

If you insist on moving your plants (they may be valuable for one reason or another), it is suggested that you first research how to move them and learn how to keep them alive at the new location. You can also get free advice from professionals.

For more information, contact your local cooperative extension service, nursery, or public botanical garden.

## Food

Don't move perishable food—those items that might deteriorate during the trip, such as frozen food. You should try to use up these items or give them away before moving day; frozen foods and other groceries weigh a lot. If you can't consume or give away all the food, contact local charitable organizations or churches.

### Books and Records

When push comes to shove, we all can weed out unnecessary books from our collections. With a move, this is in order. Books are very heavy, so moving time is an excellent opportunity to donate some of your collection to a local library or literacy program. Phone books are also heavy, but you might want to hold on to your local telephone directory—the one you depend on most for numbers. In your new home, you may find yourself in need of your old town hall or health department number. You won't have to pay for getting a number via the telephone operator if you have your old book.

Some phonograph records may also be candidates for the garbage can. Records are very heavy (it's not unusual for a box of records to weigh about 50 pounds). Ask yourself how much they mean to you. Can you transfer some of them onto tape or discard some?

### Magazines

Many of us also accumulate magazines because they contain articles we would like to read or re-read some day. Take an hour or so to skim these magazines, then clip any articles you want to save for future reading.

### Tools

Many of us have duplicate tools we don't need to move. For example, you may have screwdrivers, claw hammers, or pairs of pliers of the same size. If you ask yourself which tools are most important to you around the house and which are in the best condition, you can reduce the number of tools you need to take to your new home.

### Furniture

Furniture is expensive to move, so if you have an old couch or similar furniture you don't need, consider disposing of it. In addition, your new home may not be able to accommodate all your furniture. Construct a floor plan of your new home to determine if furniture items will fit.

### Pianos

Transporting a piano or organ to your new home can be doubly expensive. Such instruments are heavy, may be subject to a special handling charge (particularly if the mover has a lot of steps to traverse), and will require the services of a tuner to get them sounding right once they arrive. A specialist is not normally required to move a piano. Regular movers are also trained to do this.

### Pool Tables

A pool table is another expensive item to move. For safety reasons, and to save space, it cannot be shipped assembled. Instead, it must be disassembled and reassembled at the destination, with the slate going in its own wooden box. Unless you know exactly how to disassemble and assemble a pool table, you will have to hire a company that specializes in doing this.

### Clothing

The amount of clothing shipped should be reduced for a number of reasons. First, it can add more to the cost of a move than you might guess: A standard box of clothing, filled to the top, can weigh about 100 pounds. Also, you may not want clothing that has become old-fashioned, ill-fitting, or worn out.

Other items may be unnecessary in your new

home's climate. For example, it you're moving from New York to southern California, chances are you will no longer need heavy winter clothing. Nevertheless, you might want to keep some for trips.

# MOVING PETS

States have a variety of laws and regulations for the transportation of pets, so it is a good idea before moving to contact your state veterinarian's office (if you have one) or a similar agency. Some states have border inspections of animals, some have random checks, and some have no checks. Therefore, by following state laws (for your present state as well as for your new state) during an interstate move, you can avoid legal wrangles.

One should also check city, town, and county laws. Many areas have local ordinances relating to pets, particularly dogs, including limiting the number of any pets you may own. Moreover, most communities do not permit stabling of horses within city limits. There may also be minimum distance requirements between your barn and your neighbor's property, pasture-size limitations, and ordinances regarding exotic pets.

City license fees and the length of time allowed to apply for them vary from community to community; therefore, inquire as soon as possible.

## Health Certificates

In almost all states, a health certificate that includes statements on inoculations and general health must be available for inspection. Likewise, you must show proof that your dog (and in some states, your cat) has been inoculated against rabies. A veterinarian can supply you with these.

You should allow yourself sufficient time to check health requirements, and comply as needed.

## Transportation of Pets

Pets are not permitted to travel by bus or train. In general, cats and dogs may accompany the owner on an airplane, but each airline has different requirements, so you should check with the individual carrier. Those airlines that allow pets to travel with passengers require pet animals to be confined in a suitable carrier stowed under the seat. A guide dog is normally allowed to travel with its owner, but the airline must be told about it beforehand.

Pets may also be shipped via air freight. Again, requirements differ, but all call for a suitable container—one that is strong, leakproof, escapeproof, and designed for air travel. Some airlines sell such containers, and they are good investments. (Whatever container you use, it must be marked "Live Animal" in letters at least one inch high, and the top marked "This End Up.") Secure a water dish inside the container that can be filled from the outside, and tape any feeding instructions and food to the outside of the container. Of course, the airline must be advised in advance of your pet's needs.

But the most viable way to transport your pets may be with your own vehicle.

## Airline Regulations

Normally, airlines require that only one adult dog or cat be shipped per container, or two puppies or two kittens (less than six months old). If your trip involves more than one airline, check with the second airline to ensure that your arrangements comply with their regulations.

*Tip:* If you are transporting tropical fish, it's best to have a specialist assist you. Check your phone book or your local pet store for further information. Do the same for other exotic animals.

## Follow Feeding Instructions

Follow your vet's instructions for feeding your pet prior to departure. Normally, it's a good idea to feed a dog or cat no less than six hours before the flight and serve a dish of water about two hours before departure.

It is important that each pet have an identification tag clearly labeled with the names, addresses, and telephone numbers of the people responsible for the pet. If you are on the same flight as your pet, you can usually pick up the animal 60 to 90 minutes after the flight arrives. If someone else is picking up your pet, make sure that person has the waybill number.

## Traveling by Car

Traveling by car with pets can be a satisfactory experience, but there are some things to observe.

If you are taking a dog or cat, and it is not used to traveling in a car, help ease its discomfort (and yours) by taking the animal for short drives before the big trip.

Before the move, or during the trip itself, prepare an identification tag that includes your name and new address so you can get your pet back should it escape from the car.

Outside the car, your pet should be leashed.

You may want to keep your cat in a carrier, although some cats do quite well finding a niche in the car. That's fine, too, as long as it doesn't interfere with the operation of the car.

If you are going to stay at a hotel or motel overnight, make sure that it allows pets. A number of motel and auto club guides include this information, and many are available at the library.

As you travel, it's also wise to observe these cautions:

• Don't feed your pet before you start. Limit feeding to once a day, preferably in the evening, unless your vet instructs otherwise. Adhere to set walking and feeding routines. A few treats will keep your pet satisfied during the day.

• Bring along drinking water from your former house or apartment. A change of water can upset some dogs temporarily—not because the water is unhealthy, but because the animal may not be used to it.

• Keep car windows completely or partially closed so your pet can't jump or stick its head out the window. Windblown dust from open windows can score your pet's eyes and ears, and lead to infections.

• When you park the car, don't leave your pet in the vehicle during extreme temperatures—too hot or too cold. A good criterion is to imagine yourself in the car for the same period as your pet. Would it be harmful to you?

• Exercise caution if your pet is the truculent type and likely to bite someone.

## Other Rules of the Road

• Don't leave your pet alone in the motel room without notifying management. That's particularly important with dogs, who might tear up the room in protest at being left in an unfamiliar place.

• Don't walk your pet on someone else's property.

• Clip the nails of your pet before leaving to minimize the chances of damage to your car's upholstery.

• Bring along things familiar to your pet, including its water and food dishes, a toy or two, and a supply of its regular food. Other items you may need include a comb or brush, medication (including a veterinarian-prescribed sedative if your pet is likely to get too agitated), paper towels, flea and tick repellent, aerosol deodorant for motel rooms, scooper and plastic bags to clean up after your pet, and a blanket.

## Other Pet Animals

There are a variety of other pets you may want to move yourself to your new destination. These include small animals such as hamsters and gerbils, as well as birds. They all can be transported by car. You can house them in the same cages they use at home.

It is best to give them water every time you stop. (Remove their regular water container so it doesn't spill during the trip.) Small animals and birds are subject to quick dehydration, especially when the weather is hot. But you can feed them as you normally would. Birds don't take well to travel and are susceptible to drafts and sudden temperature changes. Try to keep them as calm as possible by covering their cages during the trip.

If you wish, you can also send small pets by airplane, but follow appropriate carrier regulations.

## Fish

It is important to consult with your vet or someone knowledgeable about fish before taking them with you. The tips that follow will generally serve you well, but it is best to know as many of the specifics as possible.

Fish can also be transported by car. You can take the entire aquarium with you as long as it's small (one to five gallons) and sturdy enough to resist breakage. First remove the heater hood, aerator, and anything else that can move and possibly break the glass. Plastic film should be stretched across the top and the aquarium placed in a box cushioned by newspaper. When lifting the aquarium, make sure that the box bottom is solid and that the aquarium can't fall through. It's also important to wedge the box in a place in the car where it's least likely to move.

Or you can fill a strong, leakproof bag one-third of the way (fish need air) and tie the top securely with a rubber band. Place this bag in another leakproof bag, and then both bags in a Styrofoam container, such as a cooler. The cooler will help maintain the temperature of the water for a couple of days, an important health factor for tropical fish (they do not respond well to sudden changes in temperature).

Another way to carry fish is by using something like a minnow bucket, which has a lid with holes in it. You can fill this halfway with aquarium water.

Whatever method you choose to carry fish, it is important not to have too many in one container. Give them ample room, something you can determine by asking your vet or local pet-shop owner.

Feeding fish is usually not a problem. Many species can go a week without eating anything at all.

As with other pets, it's essential to try to re-establish the fish's former environment. This means taking the aquarium accessories with you. If there are plants or snails in the aquarium, pack these in small plastic bags with a little water.

Make it a priority to get the fish into the aquarium as soon as possible after arriving at your new residence. Reconstruct the aquarium, pour in the water you took with you, add accessories, then place the fish in the tank. If the water level needs to be elevated, add tap water gradually. In some cases, you may need to investigate if the new water contains chemicals that need to be neutralized. Such neutralizers are commonly available at pet shops. You can also buy medications to add to the water, in case any fish were bruised en route.

## Horses

You can move a horse yourself, you can hire someone who specializes in moving horses, or you can ship a horse by air.

Moving a horse yourself is not just a matter of hooking a trailer to the back of your car or truck: It takes a great deal of practice. Always use trailers specifically designed for transporting horses. Such units will also have enough space in them for supplies and feed.

If the trip will take more than one day, you must plan to board your horse overnight. As you travel, make use of nearby resources—for example, fields on which the animal can graze. Your horse trailer may be allowed to stay in a parking lot. Rural communities are especially accommodating.

If necessary, a horse or pony can be stabled at reasonable rates. The key, again, is planning and knowing how much it will cost. If you do expect to stop at a stable, be prepared to produce an interstate health certificate and a statement declaring that the animal is free of equine infectious anemia.

You can also transport a horse by air. Of course, you must first check with the airline. Normally, you would be required to supply a shipping stall and perhaps ramps to get the animal on and off the plane. Also, someone must accompany the horse, and the airlines will only ship nonstop. Shipping the animal with bridle, saddle, and harness carries a separate charge.

Another way to ship a horse is with the help of a horse transporter—a company that specializes in moving horses. Such companies, which are monitored by the ICC, will make all necessary arrangements for transporting the animal. Give them at least three weeks' notice.

## Unusual Pets

If you have any special or unusual pets, your first step should be to contact your destination state to see what restrictions apply. Some states won't allow some animals to enter at all, or they have very specific rules for their handling.

You can also transport such animals by automobile or ship them by air, but again, you should make all necessary inquiries beforehand to make sure that things go smoothly.

## At Destination

While it is important to ship an animal properly, it is equally important to establish it in its new home. Cats that normally are allowed out should be confined to the house for a couple of weeks until they become used to it and recognize it as their new home territory. Otherwise, they might follow their natural instinct and try to find their way back home.

Birds are particularly sensitive to change, and they should be kept in a quiet area of the home until they settle in. Small animals such as gerbils usually have few adjustment problems, but making sure that they have their usual toys helps expedite the transition. It also helps to put food and water dishes in locations that correlate as much as possible with their former home.

## A New Veterinarian

If you can't get the name of a new vet from your old vet, there are other good sources. For a re-

---

## Facts About Transporting Animals

• Some states require that animals being brought into their jurisdictions meet certain health standards. Ask state and town officials about any requirements before you depart.

• Carefully check the requirements of the air carrier regarding the transporting of your pet before you embark. Carriers have different requirements. Special containers are required by all.

• Attached written instructions—as well as food packets—to the container the pet will be traveling in.

• When traveling by car with a cat or dog, make sure it's leashed when you get out to walk it.

• Before you plan a stopover, check with the motel to make sure they allow pets.

• Birds are particularly sensitive to travel, so keep them calm by covering their cages.

• Check with a veterinarian or other knowledgeable person to get tips on how to ship fish.

ferral, you can contact the American Animal Hospital Association, Denver West Office Park, Denver, CO 80215.

Another way to find a vet is to ask new neighbors who have pets. They can tell you the good points (as well as the bad ones) about their experience with local vets.

## IMPORTANT POINTS

- Don't overload cartons.
- Judicious use of specialized boxes, such as wardrobe cartons and mattress boxes, can make things go a lot easier.
- Use blank newsprint rather than regular newspaper.
- Mark the faces of boxes so you can easily read what they contain.
- Set up a central place (or places) for packing.
- When packing an item, remember to make sure that it is padded to reduce the chances of breakage and to minimize movement.
- Reduce the number of food items, books, records, clothing, and furniture that need to be moved.
- Check with authorities regarding the transport of any pets.

# 4

# Alternative
# Ways to Ship

IF YOU are concerned with keeping costs to a minimum on a move and don't mind a bit of inconvenience, you can use alternate carriers for some of your goods. In some instances, these carriers have rates that are lower—sometimes half the price or more—than what you'd pay to have a moving company transport the goods.

You may also find it more desirable to use an alternate carrier in special situations. Either way, here are some other choices available to you.

## POST OFFICE

If you are shipping books, the U.S. Postal Service's book rate is quite good (better than any other carrier, and generally half of what you'd pay to a mover). Although postal rates for shipping other items are generally based on weight and distance, there is just one criterion for sending books: the dimensions of the box. Whether you ship from New York to Tuscaloosa, Alabama, or from New York to White Fish, Montana, distance does not affect price. Therefore, the farther you ship books, the more you save in comparison with other carriers.

### Fourth-Class Rate

Books are shipped by what is known as special fourth-class rate. To give an idea of what you can save by using the postal service, it would cost approximately $18 to ship 65 pounds of books from Huntington, New York, to Austin, Texas. The same shipment traveling the same route by North American Van Lines would cost you around $33.

Of course, the U.S. Postal Service, like other carriers, has size and weight limitations. The weight of the shipment must be 70 pounds or less, with a girth (the distance around the widest part of the package) of less than 108 inches.

## You Should Limit Weight

When it comes to shipping books, it is important to stay within weight limits. It doesn't take too many books placed in a box before you're at the 70-pound maximum. To manage boxes more easily, it is suggested that you limit their weight to around 30 pounds. Most people can lift at least that much; lifting a 70-pound box may be too much of a strain.

Books should also be packaged correctly, so check with your local post office before you begin packing. If they're not packed according to postal guidelines, they will not be shipped.

Remember, using the post office is an economical but not very speedy method of shipping books. (Boxes can take two to three weeks to reach their destination.) If waiting time is not a disadvantage to you, give them a call.

# PRIVATE PARCEL CARRIERS

Another type of carrier that may save you money is the private parcel carrier, one of which is United Parcel Service (UPS). Ground rates for private parcel carriers—which are the cheapest—are calculated according to weight and to the total distance the packages travel. Packages must weigh less than 70 pounds and be no more than 130 inches in length, with a girth not exceeding a maximum length of 108 inches per package. The minimum charge for a package over 84 inches in girth and length combined is equal to the charge for a package weighing 30 pounds. For example, if the item you ship is very long and narrow but weighs only 10 pounds, you'd still be charged the minimum rate, which is the cost of a 30-pound package.

## Unrestricted

For price alone, the U.S. Postal Service beats UPS, at least for books. It would cost you $21.69 to ship 65 pounds of books from New York to Austin using UPS, or $3.69 more than the post office would charge (based on 1993 rates). On the other hand, UPS does not have restrictions on what you can send, and it beats the U.S. Postal Service on rates for other items.

Another advantage of UPS is that your shipment will get to its destination quicker. To send something from New York to Austin would take four business days. Also, for an additional 75 cents you can take advantage of UPS's package tracking service; you will be able to pinpoint the whereabouts of your package at any time.

## Packaging Requirements

Like other carriers, UPS has restrictions on how items may be packaged. For example, a cardboard box must be used, the package sealed with packaging tape (no other kind), and the contents cushioned.

You can have your packages picked up by UPS for a fee of $5 (for up to 70 pounds). Or you can save the $5 by taking the package to a UPS package center, if there is one near you.

UPS also has a domestic (as well as international) air freight service, but for moving it is not cost-effective.

# AIRLINES

Airlines offer a couple of ways to ship, one of which can result in solid savings: Simply carry as much as you can with you when flying to your new home. A person can generally travel with three pieces of luggage and not pay extra charges. There are, of course, size and weight limitations, but they are quite liberal.

For instance, American Airlines will allow each ticketed person to take three pieces of luggage. Two may be stored below and the third carried on board. One of the non-carry-on pieces must be no more than 62 inches in height, length, or width and can weigh no more than 70 pounds. The second piece must be no more than 55 inches in height, length, or width and no more than 70 pounds. The carry-on piece may be no more than 45 inches tall and weigh a maximum of 70 pounds.

Of course, this can add up to a lot of weight—about 210 pounds per person—but also a lot of savings. For a family of three, that means over 600 pounds would not have to be transported in the moving van. If you are paying the mover 50 cents a pound, you'd save over $300.

If you want to take extra pieces (beyond three items), it gets expensive. For example, to fly a 65-pound package from New York to Austin via United Airlines, it would cost $55.25 (about triple what your post office would charge). Northwest Airlines charges even more (about $84).

### Air Freight

Airlines also have air freight divisions, but these are not known for their savings. Generally, packages must weigh 100 pounds or less to be accepted, although heavier items can be shipped. Still, you'll have to inquire on an individual basis because there are size restrictions as well. For example, the item must be able to be loaded onto the airplane—that is, it must fit through the doors.

Northwest Airlines would not allow us to ship a cabinet that was 4 feet wide, 5 feet long, and 2 feet deep because the company can't accept anything wider than 44 inches and taller than 47 inches.

## BUSES

You can also ship by bus, but this is an expensive route, at least for shipping household goods.

According to Greyhound, a major bus carrier, a 65-pound package shipped from Huntington to Austin would cost about $76 (based on 1993 rates). In addition, it would have to be picked up at the bus station or, if a local delivery service is available, shipped to your destination at an additional cost.

However, you can save money with a bus, as you can with a plane, by taking extra luggage with you. You will be allowed to ship 100 pounds of freight per passenger and carry on two pieces for storage in the overhead rack (regardless of weight).

## RAILROAD

Amtrak is another way you can ship. Amtrak charges $28 for any package weighing up to 100 pounds. This is not much more than what UPS or the post office charges to send a 65-pound package from Huntington to Austin. Thereafter, the rate is 26 cents a pound, or $26 per hundred pounds. Such rates can usually beat those charged by moving companies.

Like any carrier, Amtrak has its restrictions. Packages may not be more than 36 inches by 36 inches in girth and length, and the maximum total weight for one shipment is 500 pounds (400 of which would be charged at a rate of 26 cents a pound). In general, though, this can save you a significant amount over movers' rates.

Note that Amtrak has restrictions on what it will ship. For example, it will not ship furniture, linens, pots and pans, dishes, or electronic items such as a television set.

Of course, you must bring your packages to the railroad station for shipment. In many cities, you can arrange to have them shipped to you at your destination, but this would hardly be cost-effective.

## SHOP AROUND

When shopping for any alternative means to ship items, explore all possibilities and do some careful calculating of costs. Most shippers have toll-free numbers, so it is not difficult or very expensive to make precise price comparisons.

Of course, you must also consider the inconveniences that may be involved in using any alternate carrier. For example, you may have to endure lugging hundreds of pounds to an airline, bus, or train terminal. On the other hand, saving a few hundred dollars may help soothe whatever gets strained.

## IMPORTANT POINTS

• Savings can be reaped by shipping books via the U.S. Postal Service or UPS.

• You can carry some items for free on an airline—potentially hundreds of dollars' worth.

• Amtrak represents another money-saving alternative for shipping goods.

• Use toll-free numbers to shop around for the best shipping buys.

# 5

# Do-It-Yourself
# Moving

THERE are advantages as well as disadvantages to making a do-it-yourself move. The following information takes both into consideration.

## SAVING MONEY

One of the big advantages of moving yourself, and the most common reason people opt for it, is the opportunity to save money. And people do save, although do-it-yourself truck companies sometimes exaggerate those claims. In price quotes, they often compare the total cost of a professional move with the cost of renting a truck, without taking related expenses into consideration.

Also, the cost of a professional move, with the vast discounts available today, may be surprisingly close to what a truck rental would cost. For example, the Paul Arpin Company estimated that it would cost $2,500 in line-haul charges to

move 5,000 pounds of household goods from Huntington, New York, to Austin, Texas. But the U-Haul company said it could rent a 24-foot truck to make the same trip for $2,200, or $300 less (without bringing in other possible costs—and, of course, you would do all of the loading and unloading). Other truck rental companies offered lower rates. Thus, careful homework can lead to big savings.

## TRUCK COST

The largest expense on a do-it-yourself rental is the cost of the truck itself, and this can vary significantly from company to company.

Basic rates also vary according to the size of the truck you rent. The rental company will provide you with this information. When you call for an estimate—and you should—just state how many rooms you have to ship. Of the five companies we contacted in 1993 for this book, four truck rental companies recommended a 24-foot truck for shipping five rooms of furniture to Austin from Huntington. Another recommended a 20-foot truck. There was roughly a $100 to $300 difference between truck rates based on size. In other words, it pays to know precisely what truck size you will need, something you may be able to determine in detailed discussions with renters. (Or, you can use the chart on page 56 to calculate the cubic footage.)

## TRAILERS

You can generally save half of what your shipment would normally cost by truck if you use a trailer. This may be practical if your shipment is

---

## Truck Rental Prices

Shopping around is the name of the game when it comes to truck rentals. There can be wide—and subtle—differences.

Trucks are rented according to the distance they'll be traveling, their size, and the number of days in your possession. In other words, you get a package: a truck of a certain size to travel so many miles in a specific number of days. You must take the package price. For example, if a company allowed you six days to reach your destination and you got there in four days, you'd still have to pay the six-day rate.

It should be emphasized that you normally can't make a trip in a truck as quickly as you can in a car. Experts in the field recommend that you should go no more than 300 miles a day when driving a good-size truck. They also say that, for a major move, you should figure on one day for loading and one day for unloading.

### Price Quotes

The following (1993) quotes are for a 24-foot truck traveling from Huntington to Austin (1,951 miles).

U-Haul had the highest package price, giving an estimate of $2,208 for the trip and allowing 2,079 free miles and nine days' travel time.

The average cost for this trip would be $245 per day. If you figure on one day for loading, one day for unloading, and seven days for driving, you would have to drive an average of 278 miles a day to stay within the contract conditions.

Ryder Truck Rental quoted a slightly lower rate of $2,099, but its daily rate was by far the highest because it would allow only seven days for the trip. That would cost you $299 per day, and you would have to drive an average of 390 miles per day.

Budget Car and Truck Rental was cheaper than both U-Haul and Ryder. It allowed 2,200 free miles at a cost of $1,867, with nine days to complete the trip. That would cost you $207 per day, and you would need to drive an average of 278 miles per day.

All three companies impose penalty and mileage charges beyond what is in the package price.

The best price, far and away, was given by Hertz Penske Truck Rental. Its price was $1,239 for eight days of travel—$1,000 less than U-Haul on a package price—and included unlimited mileage. Thus, if you wanted to lengthen your trip (by distance, not time), you would not suffer any penalties. Based on Hertz Penske's rates, the cost per day would be $158.

### Local Moves

If you are moving within the same region, then you should consider hiring a local truck company. The shorter the distance, the less you need the resources of a large company, and you will get a better price.

Additionally, it is usually easier to deal with local representatives of these companies (they are often more responsive to special needs) than with the salespeople who work the toll-free numbers at the main offices.

relatively small and convenient to haul by car. Two typical trailer sizes are:

- A 6-foot-by-12-foot trailer capable of holding up to three rooms of furniture (5 feet by 10 feet by 8 feet of storage area)
- A 5-foot-by-8-foot trailer capable of carrying up to two rooms

You can also rent even smaller trailers (for example, one with 5 feet by 5 feet by 8 feet of storage area).

## RELATED EQUIPMENT

Another consideration is the cost of the equipment involved in the move. In 1993, U-Haul charged the following equipment fees:

Appliance dolly—$10
Utility dolly—$7
Tow bar—$82
Side-view mirrors—$2 each
Rental hitch—$5
Furniture pads—$10 a dozen

You should also factor in the cost of boxes and packing materials. (See chapter 3 for information on collecting boxes for the job.)

## TRAVEL EXPENSES

Another group of costs associated with a do-it-yourself move is traveling costs.

Tolls are one travel-related cost. If the move is made by a professional mover, those costs are included in the estimate. Do-it-yourself movers, however, must pay for tolls out of their own pockets, and such costs can be higher for a truck than for a car because tolls are charged according to the number of axles on a vehicle.

### Extra Gas Cost

Gas expenses will also be higher for a truck than for a car. You can figure on the average rental truck getting about 5 miles to the gallon. If you are traveling 1,000 miles and gas costs $1.20 per gallon, it can be an expensive trip. To calculate costs, you would divide the number of miles traveled by the estimated miles per gallon. In this case, 1,000 miles divided by 5 miles per gallon equals 200 gallons of gas. At $1.20 per gallon, that comes to $240.

If you are traveling by car, figure on paying a lot less. If your car got 20 miles to the gallon, for example, it would cost about $60 to make the trip.

Incidentally, truck rental companies may claim that their vehicles can get more than 5 miles per gallon. Their estimates, however, are normally based on the mileage of empty trucks. Since your truck will be loaded with furniture, 5 miles per gallon is more realistic.

## EXTRA VEHICLES

Other costs may result from the need for another vehicle. Do-it-yourself rental trucks commonly seat just three people comfortably, so if you have a large family, you may not be able to fit everyone into the van. Alternate transportation for these family members may mean spending more money.

## FOOD AND LODGING

Costs for food and lodging are higher when traveling by truck, simply because a truck is slower than a car. The longer it takes to reach your destination, the more meals and, perhaps, lodging you require. Let's say you can average 300 miles a day in a car but only 200 miles per day in a van. That would add 100 miles per day to your itinerary and perhaps an extra day or two on the road—and extra meal and lodging costs.

## LABOR

Another disadvantage of moving yourself is the hard work involved. You have to move everything out of your house, load it onto the truck, drive the truck to your destination, and then unload it. Your muscles may not be used to such stress and strain. (It is estimated that it takes about two hours per room to load and unload a truck.)

Also, you may have plenty of help loading the truck, but what about unloading it? If you don't have enough helpers at your destination, you may have a very difficult job and may have to go to the expense of hiring someone.

## DRIVING

Driving a truck can be strenuous, too, especially if you are not experienced driving a larger

---

### Help with Unloading

One of the difficulties of moving yourself may be getting help unloading the truck at your destination. There is usually no easy solution to this, but one of the following may work:

• Arrange to have someone come with you for the sole purpose of helping you unload. This may be practical for a short trip but not for a long-distance move.

• Ask your new employer, if you have one, if he or she knows someone who might help. Perhaps some of your new coworkers will be able to lend a hand.

• Arrange for the help of a trusted person who lives relatively close to your new home.

---

vehicle. It simply doesn't handle like a car, and you have to be careful entering and leaving spaces. Moreover the problem is compounded by having to travel unfamiliar roads.

### Mechanical Problems

Another potential problem is a mechanical breakdown. You should find out what, if anything, the truck rental company will charge you in case of a breakdown or accident, or if a family member becomes sick. The trip can often take longer than anticipated, extending the time you have the truck. Ordinarily, the company will give you ample time to get to your destination, but find out what penalties, if any, apply if you're late. (One company quoted a penalty rate of $40 a day.)

Also, if you have a mechanical breakdown and the company doesn't have a repair affiliate nearby, you may have to use an unaffiliated repair station. Of course, the rental company will reimburse you for out-of-pocket repair costs, but this may take some time.

## LOW-DEMAND AREA

You should also check to see if you live in what truck rental companies call a low-demand area. If you do, you may be required to pay extra. If you are traveling into Florida, there may be an extra charge (from $175 to $350) because it is so difficult to rent trucks in that area for the return trip. (There are simply too many trucks there already, and rental companies have to send drivers to take trucks out.)

## INSURANCE

Insurance is another cost factor, and your options include cargo (damage to shipment) and collision (damage to truck) insurance. Costs vary from area to area and from company to company. For example, Budget quoted a rate of $7.50 a day for insuring belongings, with a $100 deductible that would cover up to $7,500 worth of goods.

## ADVANTAGES

One of the positive aspects of do-it-yourself moving, of course, is that you will save money, and sometimes a great deal of it, compared with a professional move. All other benefits may pale beside this central fact.

But cost is not the only advantage. Handling your own goods puts you in total control of the move. By doing it yourself, you ensure that care is taken with your possessions—assuming you know how to pack and load them properly.

## SHOPPING AROUND

Shopping around for the best price begins with knowing your load. As mentioned earlier, tell the rental company how many rooms you have to move so you can arrive at the cubic footage needed, and thus the truck size.

For one room of furniture, you would need a truck with 295 cubic feet and a 1,700-pound capacity; for two to four rooms, 600 to 750 cubic feet and a 3,600-to-3,800-pound capacity; for 5 rooms or more, 1,000 to 1,500 cubic feet and a 6,500-to-8,500-pound capacity.

## FINE-TUNE ESTIMATE

Fine-tuning your estimate can ensure that you get the right-size truck. To do this, go into each room and write down the cubic footage of each item (see Table 5.1 to determine the cubic foot-

age), then total up everything and give your estimate to the rental company.

## LOADING THE TRUCK

With do-it-yourself moving, it is important to learn proper loading techniques. Professional movers load trucks in what are known as *tiers.* These, you might say, are walls built of household goods, each independent of, yet adjacent to, the other.

There are five kinds of tiers you should keep in mind when loading a truck.

A furniture tier consists of such things as wooden chests, dressers, nightstands, coffee tables, and chairs of 18 inches to 22 inches in depth.

A wide tier is built from appliances like washers, dryers, refrigerators, sofas, and overstuffed chairs that are each about 30 inches to 36 inches wide.

A narrow tier is made with book cartons, file cabinets, bookshelves, hutch tops, crates, and the like.

A carton tier is made with general-purpose cartons and dish packs.

A rough tier is composed of outdoor furniture, bicycles, garden tools, lawn mowers, and other odd-size items.

### Heaviest Items on Bottom

A good tier is built with the heaviest items on the floor of the truck, the next heaviest on top of these, and the lightest items on the very top. The depth at the bottom of the tier should be the same as on the top.

Keeping these principles of loading in mind, load the appliances first, then the furniture, followed by the other items. Leave some space along the sides of the truck for mattresses, box springs, mirrors, and picture frames. Rolled-up rugs (rugs should always be rolled up) should

# Table 5.1 Calculating Your Furniture's Cubic Footage

## LIVING AND FAMILY ROOMS

| Article | Cubic Feet Per Piece | Number of Pieces | Cubic Feet |
|---|---|---|---|
| Bar, Portable | 15 | | |
| Bench, Fireside or Piano | 5 | | |
| Bookcase | 20 | | |
| Bookshelves, Sectional | 5 | | |
| Chair, Arm | 10 | | |
| Chair, Occasional | 15 | | |
| Chair, Overstuffed | 25 | | |
| Chair, Rocker | 12 | | |
| Chair, Straight | 5 | | |
| Clock, Grandfather | 20 | | |
| Day Bed | 30 | | |
| Desk, Small or Winthrop | 22 | | |
| Desk, Secretary | 35 | | |
| Fireplace Equipment | 5 | | |
| Foot Stool | 2 | | |
| Lamp, Floor or Pole | 3 | | |
| Magazine Rack | 2 | | |
| Music Cabinet | 10 | | |
| Piano, Baby, Gr. or Upr. | 70 | | |
| Piano, Parlor Grand | 80 | | |
| Piano, Spinet | 60 | | |
| Radio, Table | 2 | | |
| Record Player Port. | 2 | | |
| Rugs, Large Roll or Pad | 10 | | |
| Rugs, Small Roll or Pad | 3 | | |
| Sofa, 2 Cushions | 35 | | |
| Sofa, 3 Cushions | 50 | | |
| Sofa, 4 Cushions | 60 | | |
| Sofa, Sectional, per Sect. | 30 | | |
| Stereo | 20 | | |
| Stud, Couch or Hideabed | 50 | | |
| Tables, Dropl'f or Occas. | 12 | | |
| Tables, Coffee, End or Nest | 5 | | |
| Telephone Stand & Chair | 5 | | |
| Television Combination | 25 | | |
| Television or Radio Console | 15 | | |
| Television Table Model | 10 | | |

## DINING ROOM

| Article | Cubic Feet Per Piece | Number of Pieces | Cubic Feet |
|---|---|---|---|
| Bench, Harvest | 10 | | |
| Buffet | 30 | | |
| Cabinet, Corner | 20 | | |
| Cabinet, China | 25 | | |
| Chair, Dining | 5 | | |
| Server | 15 | | |
| Table, Dining | 30 | | |
| Tea Cart | 10 | | |
| Rugs, Large or Pad | 10 | | |
| Rugs, Small or Pad | 3 | | |

## BEDROOM

| Article | Cubic Feet Per Piece | Number of Pieces | Cubic Feet |
|---|---|---|---|
| Bed., Incl. Spring & Mattr. | | | |
| Bed, Double | 60 | | |
| Bed, King Size | 70 | | |
| Bed, Single or Hollywood | 40 | | |
| Bed, Rollaway | 20 | | |
| Bed, Bunk (set of 2) | 70 | | |
| Bookshelves, Sectional | 5 | | |
| Bureau, Dresser, Chest of Dr'w'rs, Chifrb. or Chifnr. | 25 | | |
| Cedar Chest | 15 | | |
| Chair, Boudoir | 10 | | |
| Chair, Straight or Rocker | 5 | | |
| Chaise Lounge | 25 | | |
| Desk, Small or Winthrop | 22 | | |
| Dresser or Vanity Bench | 3 | | |
| Dresser Double (Mr. & Mrs.) | 50 | | |
| Night Table | 5 | | |
| Rug, Large or Pad | 10 | | |
| Rug, Small or Pad | 3 | | |
| Vanity Dresser | 20 | | |
| Wardrobe, Small | 20 | | |
| Wardrobe, Large | 40 | | |

## NURSERY

| Article | Cubic Feet Per Piece | Number of Pieces | Cubic Feet |
|---|---|---|---|
| Bathinette | 5 | | |
| Bed, Youth | 30 | | |
| Chair, Child's | 3 | | |
| Chair, High | 5 | | |
| Chest | 12 | | |
| Chest, Toy | 5 | | |
| Crib, Baby | 10 | | |
| Table, Child | 5 | | |
| Pen, Play | 10 | | |
| Rug, Large or Pad | 10 | | |
| Rug, Small or Pad | 3 | | |

## KITCHEN

| Article | Cubic Feet Per Piece | Number of Pieces | Cubic Feet |
|---|---|---|---|
| Breakfast, Suite Chairs | 5 | | |
| Breakfast Table | 10 | | |
| Chair, High | 5 | | |
| Ironing Board | 2 | | |
| Kitchen Cabinet | 30 | | |
| Roaster | 5 | | |
| Serving Cart | 15 | | |
| Stool | 3 | | |
| Table | 5 | | |
| Utility Cabinet | 10 | | |
| Vegetable Bin | 3 | | |

## APPLIANCES (Large)

| Article | Cubic Feet Per Piece | Number of Pieces | Cubic Feet |
|---|---|---|---|
| Air Conditioner, Window | 30 | | |
| Dehumidifier | 10 | | |
| Dishwasher | 20 | | |
| Dryer, Electric or Gas | 25 | | |
| Freezer: (Cu. Capacity) | | | |
| 10 or less | 30 | | |
| 11 to 15 | 45 | | |
| 16 and over | 60 | | |
| Ironer or Mangle | 12 | | |
| Range, Electric or Gas | 30 | | |
| Refrigerator (Cu. Capacity) | | | |
| 6 cu. ft. or less | 30 | | |
| 7 to 10 cu. ft. | 45 | | |
| 11 cu. ft. and over | 60 | | |
| Vacuum Cleaner | 5 | | |
| Washing Machine | 25 | | |

## PORCH, OUTDOOR FURNITURE & EQUIPMENT

| Article | Cubic Feet Per Piece | Number of Pieces | Cubic Feet |
|---|---|---|---|
| Barbecue or Port. Grill | 10 | | |
| Bath, Bird | 5 | | |
| Chairs, Lawn | 5 | | |
| Chairs, Porch | 10 | | |
| Clothes Line | 5 | | |
| Clothes Dryer Rack | 5 | | |
| Garden Hose and Tools | 10 | | |
| Glider or Settee | 20 | | |
| Ladder, Extension | 10 | | |
| Lawn Mower (Hand) | 5 | | |
| Lawn Mower (Power) | 15 | | |
| Lawn Mower (Riding) | 35 | | |
| Leaf Sweeper | 5 | | |
| Outdoor Child's Slide | 10 | | |
| Outdoor Child's Gym | 20 | | |
| Outdoor Drying Racks | 5 | | |
| Outdoor Swings | 30 | | |
| Picnic Table | 20 | | |
| Picnic Bench | 5 | | |
| Porch Chair | 10 | | |
| Rocker, Swing | 15 | | |
| Roller, Lawn | 15 | | |
| Rug, Large | 7 | | |
| Rug, Small | 3 | | |
| Sand Box | 10 | | |
| Settee | 20 | | |
| Spreader | 1 | | |
| Table | 10 | | |
| Umbrella | 5 | | |
| Wheel Barrow | 8 | | |

## MISCELLANEOUS

| Article | Cubic Feet Per Piece | Number of Pieces | Cubic Feet |
|---|---|---|---|
| Ash or Trash Can | 7 | | |
| Basket (Clothes) | 5 | | |
| Bicycle | 10 | | |
| Bird Cage & Stand | 5 | | |
| Card Table | 1 | | |
| Cabinet, Filling | 20 | | |
| Carriage, Baby | 20 | | |
| Chairs, Folding | 1 | | |
| Clothes, Hamper | 5 | | |
| Cot, Folding | 10 | | |

## MISCELLANEOUS

| Article | Cubic Feet Per Piece | Number of Pieces | Cubic Feet |
|---|---|---|---|
| Desk, Office | 30 | | |
| Fan | 5 | | |
| Fernery or Plant Stands | 10 | | |
| Foot Lockers | 5 | | |
| Garbage Cans | 7 | | |
| Golf Bag | 2 | | |
| Heater, Gas or Electric | 5 | | |
| Incinerator | 10 | | |
| Metal Shelves | 5 | | |
| Ping Pong Table | 20 | | |
| Pool Table | 40 | | |
| Power Tools | 20 | | |
| Sewing Machine | 10 | | |
| Sled | 2 | | |
| Step Ladder | 5 | | |
| Suitcase | 5 | | |
| Table, Utility | 5 | | |
| Tackle Box | 1 | | |
| Tool Chest | 10 | | |
| Tricycle | 5 | | |
| Wagon, Child's | 5 | | |
| Waste Paper Basket | 2 | | |
| Work Bench | 20 | | |

also be placed along the sides but under the other side items.

### Tie off Tiers

Every 10 feet or so, tie off the tiers. The enemy of a good loading job is movement, so you want to guard against this.

If possible, don't leave any gaps between items, and be sure to wrap anything that isn't in a carton (use a mover's pad or blanket). Your goal should be to pack so there is minimal movement. Ideally, you should also place cartons at the back of the truck and seal off the load with a mattress. If any of the tiers lean, they should be toward the front of the van.

### Safe Lifting

To prevent injuries, it is important to be careful when lifting heavy items. Following these suggestions can help:

- Always keep your back straight.
- When lifting something off the floor, bend your knees and lift straight up.
- When taking something large out of a house, two people should be involved—one to guide, the other to push.
- Don't overexert yourself. If an item is heavy, *get help.* Then draw as close to the item as you can, so as not to hyperextend your arms, and lift together.

## IMPORTANT POINTS

- When calculating the total cost of a do-it-yourself move, be sure to factor in all possible extra expenses such as gas, food, and lodging in the event the trip takes longer than anticipated.
- Get bids from several rental companies. The differences can be significant.
- Carefully load the truck to minimize movement.
- Be careful when lifting anything heavy, so as not to hurt yourself. Keep your back straight when lifting something off the floor.

# 6

# Intrastate
# Moving

MOVING intrastate, or within the confines of a particular state, must be approached with the same caution as an interstate move—perhaps even more. One reason is that unlike interstate moves, intrastate moves are not monitored as closely. The ICC is not involved, and state regulations are inconsistent.

## WEIGHT, HOURLY, OR BINDING RATES

In general, local or intrastate moves are priced either by weight or by the hour. If the total distance of the move is less than 40 or 50 miles, the cost is generally calculated by the hour. Thus, you won't know what the final expense will be until the move is complete. You may be able to get an experienced estimator to come to your home and estimate how many hours it will take to move your belongings.

A written estimate is highly recommended. In New York State, if you get a written estimate for an hourly rated move and the cost exceeds this by 25 percent (10 percent for a weight-distance move), the mover is required to deliver the goods at your request upon payment of the probable cost plus 25 percent.

Weight-rated moves are usually for longer trips, and the charges are based on the weight of the goods and the distance they will travel. The intrastate mover will quote a rate per 100 pounds, just as an interstate mover would.

And just as you cannot know the cost of an interstate move until all goods are loaded onto the truck, the same is true of an intrastate move. Some movers offer a contract covering all charges for a set rate called the *binding price*. Anything offered in this binding price must be written in the mover's tariff, including all services the mover is to provide.

Of course, if you hire someone to pack your belongings, you can expect to pay for both the labor involved and the packing materials. Intrastate and interstate moves are similar in this respect.

## STATE REGULATIONS

Some states follow general rules and regulations, but some do not. Alaska, Arizona, Colorado, Delaware, Hawaii, Maine, New Mexico, and Vermont have no regulations at all.

With intrastate moves, companies are free to do whatever they want—there is no regulating agency like the ICC. There may be controls at some local level, but most communities do not have the resources to spend on policing.

In 1991 the New York State Department of Transportation did a survey of 42 regulated states to determine just what kind of licensing, penalties, and so forth were in place around the nation. They received responses from 39 states; three chose not to participate. In general, most states indicated that there were very weak regulations governing intrastate movers. And even in those states with licensing requirements, there are relatively few licensed companies.

Furthermore, many of the states have no system to process claims or investigate movers who overcharge, and they have no enforcement mechanism. When fines are levied against companies, they are generally very small. For example, Minnesota fined movers a grand total of $600 in 1991. Iowa, Kentucky, Louisiana, Missouri, Oregon, and some other states did not fine movers a single dollar that year.

### Tough States

A few states, however, assert greater control. In 1991 California fined movers $75,000; Texas's fines totaled $1.3 million, although this figure includes fines levied against all transportation companies, not just movers.

All of this emphasizes one central point: You must take great care to protect yourself when hiring anyone for an intrastate or local move. Do not depend on the government to come to your rescue once the damage is done. Protect yourself before you move. To do this, you can follow the same tips for hiring an interstate mover.

• Contact the state agency that controls household moves in your state, if one exists, to see if the mover is licensed and insured. (These agencies are listed in Appendix A.) Get literature that will provide details on moving.

• Contact three or four movers, preferably ones that have been used by friends, neighbors, relatives—any reliable sources—and invite bids.

• Check with the local consumer affairs agency for complaints. If you see a pattern of complaints against particular movers, cross them off your list.

• Get estimates in writing, including all details of the move.

• Visit the premises of the company you are thinking of hiring to see what kind of operation they run and what kind of equipment they have.

• Be present when the inventory is being taken, list any damaged items on the inventory form, and get statements from movers that all other items are in good condition.

• Watch the loading of your goods. That forces the movers to be more careful.

• Be present at the unloading, calling attention to any damage to your goods. Have the driver initial the inventory form to indicate damage. If the driver won't initial it, make a note on your copy.

• Do not sign off on anything until the delivery is complete.

## CUTTING COSTS

To cut costs on an intrastate move, follow the same recommendations for an interstate move.

• Reduce the number of items you have to move.

## Table 6.1 State Regulation of Movers

| State* | Number of Licensed Movers | Number of Complaints Against Licensed/ Unlicensed Movers | Power to Resolve Loss or Damage/ Overcharge | Fines Paid by Movers (1991) | Police Powers |
|---|---|---|---|---|---|
| AL | 62 | 20/200 | No/Yes | $1,000 | Yes |
| AR | 41 | 5/10 | No/Yes | N.A. | Yes |
| CA | 1,200 | 2,500/500–700 | No/Yes | $75,000 | Yes |
| CT | 140 | 20/20 | No/Yes | $0 | No |
| GA | N.A. | N.A./N.A. | No/Yes | $4,000 | Yes |
| IL | 386 | 200/150 | No/No | N.A. | Yes |
| IN | 90 | 10/10 | No/Yes | N.A. | Yes |
| IA | 100 | 25/50 | No/Yes | $0 | Yes |
| KS | 75 | 15/10 | No/Yes | $0 | Yes |
| KY | 175 | N.A./N.A. | Yes/Yes | N.A. | Yes |
| LA | 60 | 10/4 | Yes/Yes | $0 | No |
| MA | 375 | 100/50 | No/Yes | N.A. | Yes |
| MI | 160 | 50/25 | No/Yes | $1,000 | Yes |
| MN | 250 | 30/50 | No/Yes | $600 | Yes |
| MS | 51 | 3/N.A. | No/No | N.A. | N.A. |
| MO | 85 | N.A./N.A. | No/No | $0 | No |
| MT | 30 | 2/10 | No/No | $0 | Yes |
| NE | 56 | 20/30 | No/Yes | $0 | Yes |
| NV | 19 | N.A./N.A. | No/Yes | N.A. | Yes |
| NH | N.A. | N.A./N.A. | Yes/Yes | N.A. | Yes |
| NJ | 400 | 300/10 | Yes/Yes | N.A. | No |
| NY | 750 | 290/115 | No/Yes | $6,800 | No |
| NC | 150 | N.A./N.A. | N.A./Yes | N.A. | N.A. |
| ND | 25 | 3/0 | No/No | N.A. | Yes |
| OH | N.A. | N.A./N.A. | No/Yes | N.A. | No |
| OK | N.A. | 100/30 | Yes/No | $0 | Yes |
| OR | 175 | 50/35 | No/Yes | $2,000 | No |
| PA | 40 | 100/50 | No/Yes | N.A. | No |
| RI | 100 | 50/40 | No/Yes | $10,000 | Yes |
| SC | 83 | N.A./N.A. | No/Yes | N.A. | Yes |
| SD | 27 | 20/2 | No/Yes | N.A. | No |
| TN | 39 | 25/25 | Yes/Yes | N.A. | N.A. |
| TX | N.A. | 125/125 | No/Yes | $1.3 million | No |
| UT | 18 | 5/5 | No/Yes | N.A. | Yes |
| VA | 150 | 30/30 | No/Yes | N.A. | Yes |
| WA | 267 | 100/100 | No/Yes | N.A. | Yes |
| WV | N.A. | 10/10 | No/Yes | N.A. | Yes |
| WI | N.A. | N.A./N.A. | No/No | N.A. | Yes |
| WY | 34 | 6/6 | No/No | N.A. | No |

*Only 39 states responded to the survey.
*Source:* New York State Department of Transportation

• Pursue the best estimate, but beware of "low-ball" bids.

• Pack as much as possible yourself with your own scavenged boxes.

• Ship selected items (e.g., books) by alternative means.

## DO IT YOURSELF

Hiring a rental van and doing the job yourself makes more sense for a local, intrastate move than for an interstate move because:

• You probably won't have to drive as far on an intrastate move. In addition, it won't be as physically draining, and you won't have to include in your budget such things as motel expenses and eating out. It will be proportionately cheaper, too.

• The likelihood of your getting help to unload the truck is greater.

## IMPORTANT POINTS

As with interstate moves, there are various types of intrastate moves: weight rated, or based on a charge per 100 pounds; hourly rated, where you hire movers for a certain amount of time; and binding, where you get a rate that's locked in. In addition:

• You will not know the final cost on a weight-rated or hourly move until the move is completed.

• Get the names of movers from reliable sources.

• Check out potential movers with any state regulatory agency.

• Obtain estimates from three or four movers.

• Get everything in writing.

• Visit the business premises of the company you're thinking of hiring to see what kind of an operation they run.

• It will generally be less expensive to hire a rental truck for an intrastate move than for an interstate move.

# 7

# International Moving

ALTHOUGH you would follow many of the same steps in preparing for domestic and international moves, there are important considerations unique to moving abroad. First of all, you have to be cautious about much more. One executive from Bekins Van Lines estimated that major problems occur in about 15 percent of international moves. For example, some people arrive in a country and have to wait months for their shipment to arrive. And there are numerous instances in which people have chosen a financially unstable or dishonest company. Sometimes their goods are held hostage until they pay a higher fee than was originally negotiated.

## KNOW WHO YOU'RE HIRING

The core of the problem is that people hire international movers who do not—or cannot—

see their moves through to the end. In fact, the agent you hire may have little or no experience with an international move, even though he or she seemingly represents a big company.

## PACKING AND LOADING PROBLEMS

Problems with international moves can occur if goods are packed or loaded incorrectly into containers commonly used to ship household goods. An agent may be knowledgeable about packing and loading goods for an interstate move, but international preparations are quite different. Shipments are likely to travel much farther, be subject to greater temperature extremes, and endure much greater stress. Thus, specific experience is needed to keep shipments intact, and if the mover doesn't have that experience, you can be in deep trouble.

Incidentally, if you pack goods yourself to save some money, consult with the mover beforehand.

## FREIGHT FORWARDER PROBLEMS

Another problem can occur when the agent/ mover hires what is known as a *freight forwarder*. The agent is then responsible only for picking up the goods at your house and unloading them at the dock. From that point on, the move is handled by the freight forwarder. The forwarder is paid a fee by the agent to arrange for space on a ship, the most common way goods are transported abroad. Agents contract with forwarders for one reason: rock-bottom prices. What the local agent may not know or care about is that many of these forwarders operate on a small (or nonexistent) financial base. Anyone who has access to a telephone and a fax machine can start a forwarding company.

Hence, such freight forwarders may not care about your shipment, or they may only be interested in cutting corners to make a dollar. They may also have to cut corners because of the low prices they quote, so they can't afford to provide better service. For example, you may want your goods to arrive in Birmingham, England, on September 20 or so, but the freight forwarder may not ship them until October 20 if shipping at a later date will save the forwarder money.

And then there is the problem of finding a reliable *destination agent*. This party is responsible for the final delivery of your goods, as well as for getting them through customs. One important fact, too, is that the destination agent is normally chosen by the freight forwarder. If the freight forwarder chooses a bad destination agent, or if the destination agent doesn't get paid, you may be caught in the middle of the dispute—and your goods held until the matter is resolved. There is no way of knowing what kind of care your goods will receive in the meantime.

## PICKING A COMPANY

The process of picking a company for your international move should therefore be a very thorough one.

As with interstate or intrastate moves, you should get four or five companies involved in bidding, but only ones that have heavy experience in international moves.

Contact international movers recommended by friends or relatives or people you know who have moved abroad. Another possible source is a traffic manager from a large company. Such individuals deal with movers on a regular basis, and they could give you the names of some reliable people.

Perhaps the best way to find an international mover is to contact companies that have authority from the ICC to make interstate moves—not agents, but van lines. Such companies know that even though the ICC has no legal authority to get involved in international moves, complaints about any aspect of their business may result in the ICC looking extra hard into their interstate activities.

When it comes to international moves, bigger may indeed be better. Atlas, Bekins, Paul Arpin, United, North American, and Allied all make international moves, and they have extensive experience in the field.

## FOLLOW INTERSTATE PROCEDURES

Whatever method you choose in hiring an international mover, check out the company for current interstate authority, as detailed in chapter 1. If the mover does have authority, that's a good sign, but you must also quiz the salespeople closely on their international experience.

## HOW WILL GOODS BE PACKED?

A true test of a company's concern for your goods is the way goods are packed. When shopping for a company, ask each representative how your goods will be packed.

The best packing method involves putting items directly into large wooden containers ("vaults"), which are then shipped. The entire process is known as *pack and load*. Some movers may want to bring your goods back to their warehouses before containerizing them, but you should not allow this. The basic moving rule applies: The more your goods are handled, the greater the chance of damage.

In addition, the farther a shipment travels, the more susceptible it is to damage. Since it is likely to travel farther for an international move than for an interstate move, all the more reason for containerization.

## COSTS

International moves are priced by weight—per 100 pounds—and volume, which is important because space is limited on planes and ships. When comparing movers' costs, make sure their quotes are based on the same amount of weight and volume. Also, make sure each mover will be taking you the same distance, door-to-port, or door-to-door.

The actual cost of an international move can be surprisingly small. One mover said that you could move from New York City to Amsterdam more cheaply than you could move from New York City to San Francisco. The price depends on the ship rates, routes, help at destination, and other factors.

This might not be true, however, if you were moving from New York City to Sierra Leone. This move, because of limited help, limited ship routes, and limited space availability, would probably be quite expensive.

## BINDING PRICE GUARANTEE

As with interstate moves, shopping around should yield good discounts. Most international moves go by ship, but some rely on airlines. Transporting your goods by plane to some countries (such as those in South America) can be cheaper than by boat.

Some movers can give you a binding price to certain locations overseas. As with an interstate move, this price will include all the extra charges. Therefore, you should ask companies about this. With a nonbinding price, you have to make very sure you know all that is potentially involved.

One cost a mover can't give you is the customs duties at your destination. They vary a great deal, and no one can know precisely what they will be until the customs officer examines the shipment.

## INSURANCE

Valuation on your goods in an international move is similar to domestic valuation, but with one important distinction: The cost of insurance is a lot more expensive, up to triple what it would cost in the United States. The reason? The move is a lot riskier.

## PICKING THE MOVER

As mentioned, you must take great care in selecting an international mover. It is important to follow through with your research. You want to pick a mover who has experience moving internationally and, as such, has a strong chain of contacts stretching from your door in America to the door in your new home. The company you hire may not have salaried employees in foreign countries, but it will have contacts who can do the job.

Before you leave the United States, we recommend that you learn when your shipment will be arriving at its destination. Once you reach the country of your new residence, immediately contact the destination agent and ask him or her to inform you when your shipment comes in. In addition, ask the agent to provide the name of at least one English-speaking person, if necessary, who will be involved in the unloading of your goods (the destination agent is usually not present).

## GETTING YOUR HOUSE READY

Once you know the arrival time of your household goods, prepare your house for the delivery. Complete all cleaning and decorating, and make sure all utilities are operating. A floor plan helps, particularly if color coded. Use a different color for each of the rooms on the plan, and then make corresponding marks on the inventory sheet to show where each item belongs. It's a simple plan that will allow the delivery crew to place the goods in the right rooms without needing to be fluent in English.

You should also alert the destination agent, if he or she doesn't know already, of the physical configurations of the residence. This way, the agent can be prepared for any problems. In other words, alert the agent to the same kinds of things you would notify an interstate or intrastate mover about. These include:
- long carries
- whether hoisting is needed
- if parking permits are required
- the presence of a long, narrow driveway

## GREETING THE MOVERS

A helpful, friendly attitude can also facilitate a move. Get introduced to everyone in the destination agent's crew, then give them a grand tour of the house. Show the van driver or supervisor a copy of the floor plan so they know exactly where you want things placed. As with domestic moves, stay around while the goods are being unloaded, being as helpful as you can.

After the items are unloaded, note any damage, making sure that the crew supervisor or van driver signs off on it. You will be required to sign the inventory sheet, too. For unpacked cartons, check for tears, rips, or dents. If boxes show signs of damage, leave them in that condition and notify the mover.

## UNPACK AS SOON AS POSSIBLE

Unpack your goods as soon as possible. For liability coverage to be valid, claims have to be filed within a certain period of time (times differ from company to company, but you need to file an international claim much sooner than you do an interstate claim). For example, to file a claim with Atlas Van Lines International, unpacking should be completed within 21 days of delivery.

When unpacking, open the boxes containing the fragile items first. Then unpack the nonfragile items, noting any loss or damage as you go down the inventory sheet. Be specific in your notations. Don't just write that something is broken; state exactly in what way. In the case of a cracked vase, you might note that "vase has a 6-inch crack near the handle."

To file a claim, you will need a claim form. The destination agent can usually provide one. If you don't receive one, write directly to the van line. The form requires you to be specific as to the damage and also provide the inventory number, year the article was purchased, original purchase price, and amount you are claiming (see chapter 8 for more information on filing claims).

Claims can be settled in 90 to 120 days if you have a moving representative's initials next to your comments on the inventory form.

# FOREIGN RESIDENCY REQUIREMENTS

There are a variety of documents you should obtain to ensure easy entrance into another country.

A passport will be required for each family member entering any country other than Mexico or Canada. To remain in the country, residency visas will be required, and a work permit for conducting business (getting one may be difficult). To obtain these documents (through federal and state courts, the U.S. Passport Agency, or your local post office), you must:

• Supply proof of citizenship. If you were born in the United States, you need either a birth or baptismal record. If naturalized, you need naturalization papers.

• Show some identification, such as a driver's license, business ID, or an old passport.

• Pay the appropriate fee.

## Other Documents

As you might expect, more than a passport is required to enter another country. In advance of the move (at least three months), make sure you have the right documentation by checking with a consulate of the country you plan to enter. You may be advised to secure the following:

• *Visa.* Some countries require an entry form, which is what a visa is.

• *Work permit.* Many countries require this before you can begin work, and you must usually have received a job offer before you can receive such a permit.

• *Residency permit.* If your move is perma-

nent, or you are going to live in another country for a long time, this permit is often required.

• *Immunization certificates.* Although most countries do not require that people be vaccinated before coming in, it may be something you want to do for your family's sake and for yourself as a hedge against disease, especially when entering a developing country.

Vaccination forms can be picked up from your local health department or passport office. Some health departments also give free shots. Have a copy of your vaccination record with you when entering another country.

Contact the consulate of the country you're going to enter for details on what its rules and regulations are regarding what you may bring in. As mentioned, this can vary greatly. If there is no consulate near where you live, contact the U.S. Customs Service for information. The address is:

U.S. Customs Service
2100 K Street NW
Washington, DC 20036
Or you can write for the free booklet *Know Before You Go* at:
U.S. Customs Service
P.O. Box 7407
Washington, DC 20036

For customs purposes, it's a good idea to make an itemized list of your possessions as early as possible. Indicate their value, serial numbers, etc., just as you would for an interstate or intrastate move.

Some movers, such as Bekins and Atlas, also provide free literature profiling the religions and customs of many different countries. Libraries also carry videos and travel guides.

# LEGAL MATTERS

There are a variety of legal matters you should take care of before you move. For instance, you should:

• Give someone power of attorney. This

**Table 7.1 Example of International Guidelines: Chile**

# IMPORTING PERSONAL PROPERTY INTO CHILE

Importation of household goods into Chile may be accomplished by anyone. There is no restriction as to the quantity or value of such importations, and household goods importations can be made in one or more shipments or from one or more origin points.

## DUTY-FREE ENTRY IS PERMITTED FOR THE FOLLOWING GOODS:

*   Travel articles, clothing, and electric appliances used for personal care.
*   Shipments and/or articles previously exported from Chile.
*   Effects for diplomats, administrative employees of diplomatic entities, employees of international organizations, and Chilean nationals returning from diplomatic assignment overseas.

Household goods and personal effects (other than the aforementioned) are subject to duties and/or taxes. The current rate of duty is 15% of the CIF (Cost-Insurance-Freight) value of the articles. A value added tax of 18% of the combined CIF value plus the duties will also be assessed. This is subject to change without notice.

**AUTOMOBILES:**    Only Chilean nationals returning from an overseas diplomatic assignment, foreign diplomats, administrative employees of such diplomats, and employees of international organizations may import a **used** vehicle. Duty payable will depend on the motor capacity (cc's). **New** vehicles are subject to authorization of the **Banco Central.** Importation of vehicles is not recommended due to high importation costs.

## PROHIBITED/RESTRICTED ARTICLES:

*   Soil, although plants may enter with a phytosanitary certificate legalized by the Consulate.

*   Dogs and cats must have a sanitation vaccination and rabies certificate, both legalized by the Consulate.
*   Movies and video cassettes will be retained in customs and their importation is subject to the determination of the Censorship department upon revision.
*   Alcohol and foodstuffs must have approval from the Agricultural Livestock Service (Servicio Agricola Ganadero) and the National Health Service (Servicio Nacional de Salud).
*   Arms, ammunition, and dangerous objects require authorization from the corresponding Military Garrison (Guarnicion Militar).
*   Precious metal objects are treated the same as household goods if found to be in reasonable amounts.
*   Medicines, narcotics, and drugs are strictly prohibited unless shipper is able to furnish a medical certificate indicating the need and a prescription for use. Also, must obtain approval from the National Health Service (Servicio Nacional de Salud).

## DOCUMENTATION REQUIREMENTS:

**For household goods:** original B/L or AWB, endorsed. Inventory, an appraised listing signed by the consignee indicating trademarks, models, series or types, constitution of materials or fiber, and year of acquisition. Passports of **all** family members (it is best to provide passports of all members, regardless of age as this may lower the duty). Chilean nationals must have RUT (Chilean identification card). If returning to Chile, departure documents must be presented.

**For automobiles:** original endorsed B/L plus vehicle identification certificate, purchase invoice, ownership certificate, international police certificate, final cost certificate, internal taxes, passport and RUT.

means that you name a person to act on your behalf while you are gone. Such an individual may be asked to complete the sale of your house or to rent, lease, or otherwise manage property you have in the United States.

• Update your will. A major lifestyle change like moving abroad should prompt you to review your current will.

• Appoint a legal guardian for your children in case you are in an accident. Such a person would be authorized to care for your minor children.

# FINANCIAL MATTERS

You can consult with your accountant or banker for advice on how to resolve any financial matters affected by your move, but among the things you might want to do are:

• Pay any state, federal, and local taxes you now owe.

• Obtain a certified letter from each of your credit sources.

• Arrange for automatic transfer of your funds from your old bank to your new bank.

• Keep a safe-deposit box in the United States. Leave the key to the box with the bank, along with a letter stating who is authorized to have access to the box.

# ELECTRIC SYSTEMS

Before leaving, find out which electric system is in use in your new home. Homes in the United States operate on 120-volt, 60-cycle alternating current. Other countries, however, may use 200-to-400-volt, 50-cycle current, which may be alternating current or direct current.

To find out if your electric devices will be compatible, check the plates on the backs of the devices or simply inquire at the consulate of the country you're entering. You may need to use plug converters or some other modification to use your appliances. But converting appliances can be expensive compared with just buying replacements in your new country.

## IMPORTANT POINTS

• Even though an agent is affiliated with a big interstate or intrastate mover, he or she may not have international experience. You should conduct a thorough investigation.

• Discounts are available on international moves, but they rarely match discounts for interstate moves.

• Hire only a company that will have all the resources necessary to make an international move.

• Find out which items carry heavy-duty taxes and which items are not allowed in the country you're going to.

• Take care of legal and financial matters before moving. Give someone you trust power of attorney.

# 8

# Filing
a Claim

STICKS is a slang term in the moving industry that refers to a shipment of household goods. Sometimes that term can also describe the condition of your goods after a move. According to an official from the Household Goods Carriers' Bureau, roughly one out of every four shipments incurs some damage, and some experts say the figure is higher. The overall reason is simple. As one highly experienced mover put it, "Household goods were simply not designed for travel."

This being the case, you want to ensure as much as possible that your goods are protected against damage. However, you also want to protect yourself in the event damage should occur.

There are various types of insurance available for shippers of household goods (see chapter 2), but there is a crucial difference between what carriers offer and what is offered by insurance companies. In the case of the latter, you don't have to prove liability. But with valuation insurance (the kind movers offer), you do.

Therefore, to prove your claim, you need to provide proof not only that damage occurred but that the mover caused it. You have to establish a prima facie case. It may sound pessimistic, but it's fair to assume that some of your goods will be damaged in a move. That's why you must have proof that you sustained a loss, and that the shipper is liable.

## INVENTORY GOODS

The best way to prove that items were damaged is to first show that they were undamaged when the move began. The way to do this is to record their condition on the inventory form the movers will bring the day they arrive at your house. They will go from room to room, writing down which items are being moved and which are not, and they will also note any damge to any of the items.

You should accompany the movers on this inventory and ask to see the form whenever it is convenient for both of you. To note damage, they will use abbreviations such as the following, which are known in the trade as *exception symbols.*

| | |
|---|---|
| **BE**—bent | **MI**—mildew |
| **BR**—broken | **MO**—moth-eaten |
| **BU**—burned | **R**—rubbed |
| **CH**—chipped | **RU**—rusted |
| **CU**—contents and condition unknown | **SC**—scratched |
| | **SH**—short |
| | **SO**—soiled |
| **D**—dented | **T**—torn |
| **L**—loose | **W**—badly worn |
| **M**—marred | **Z**—cracked |

### Location Symbols

In addition to the exception symbols, the driver will use *location symbols,* which indicate where the damage is located on each item. For example:

**1**—means *arm*
**2**—means *bottom*
**3**—means *corner*
**4**—means *front*

During the inspection of the goods, the driver might write: "L1 brown sofa"—meaning the brown sofa has a loose arm.

If you disagree with any description, note it not only on your copy of the inventory but, most important, on the driver's copy. You don't want to be in the position of claiming damage and having the mover deny your claim because the inventory sheet lists the damage as preexisting.

## WHAT'S GOING—AND WHAT ISN'T

Make sure that the driver has noted what is being moved and what isn't. You don't want to arrive at your destination and find that something is missing, only to discover later on that the item has not even been accounted for on the inventory.

Incidentally, since a lot of your goods will already have been packed in boxes when the movers arrive, it would not be practical for them to open each box and examine the contents. Instead, the movers mark the boxes "PBO," meaning "packed by owner." Ostensibly, this would make you liable if damage occurs, but in fact, if the movers take the box on the truck and the contents are damaged, the company will be liable.

## BE PRESENT AT UNLOADING

You should be present not only at the loading of your goods but also at the unloading, to see how your belongings survived the trip. If you see any crushed or damaged boxes, open them immediately to see what damage has been done. Make note on the inventory form—yours and the mover's copy—of the condition of each item. If there is damage, hold on to the item as well as the crushed box.

## ITEMS OF EXTRAORDINARY VALUE

Items deemed "of extraordinary value" (those worth over $100 per pound each) must be detailed on a separate inventory form. If this is not done and damage occurs, your claim will only be paid at the rate of $100 per pound, no matter how much valuation you placed on them. You may have insured some jewelry for $5,000, for example, but if the items are not listed on a separate inventory, the carrier would be liable for only $100 per pound.

Also, make sure that you have a legible copy of the inventory, that it is completely filled out, and that the carrier has a copy. To ensure the

# Table 8.1 Household Goods Descriptive Inventory

| | DESCRIPTIVE SYMBOLS | | EXCEPTION SYMBOLS | | | LOCATION SYMBOLS | |
|---|---|---|---|---|---|---|---|
| B/W - BLACK & WHITE TV | DBO - DISASSEMBLED BY OWNER | BE - BENT | D - DENTED | M - MARRED | SC - SCRATCHED | 1. Arm | 8. Right |
| C - COLOR TV | PB - PROFESSIONAL BOOKS | BR - BROKEN | F - FADED | MI - MILDEW | SH - SHORT | 2. Bottom | 9. Side |
| CP - CARRIER PACKED | PE - PROFESSIONAL EQUIPMENT | BU - BURNED | G - GOUGED | MO - MOTHEATEN | SO - SOILED | 3. Corner | 10. Top |
| PBO - PACKED BY OWNER | PP - PROFESSIONAL PAPERS | CH - CHIPPED | L - LOOSE | R - RUBBED | T - TORN | 4. Front | 11. Veneer |
| CD - CARRIER DISASSEMBLED | MCU - MECHANICAL CONDITION | CU - CONTENTS & CONDITION | | RU - RUSTED | W - BADLY WORN | 5. Left | 12. Edge |
| | UNKNOWN | UNKNOWN | | | Z - CRACKED | 6. Legs | 13. Center |
| | | | | | | 7. Rear | 14. Inside |

NOTE: THE OMISSION OF THESE SYMBOLS INDICATES GOOD CONDITION EXCEPT FOR NORMAL WEAR

| ITEM NO. | CR. REF. | ARTICLES | CONDITION AT ORIGIN | EXCEPTIONS (IF ANY) AT DESTINATION |
|---|---|---|---|---|
| 1 | | 3,1 CTN | CP | |
| 2 | | 3,1 | | |
| 3 | | 3,1 | | |
| 4 | | 1,5 CTN | | |
| 5 | | Dish Pack | CP | |
| 6 | | Washer | MCU Control Panel Dented Top ≥,R,4,5,8,9 | |
| 7 | | Dryer | MCU SC, R, 10, SC, R, M, 4, 5, 8, 9 | |
| 8 | | Laundry Basket | W | |
| 9 | | Up. to Vacuum | MCU W, L, | |
| 0 | | Ironing Board | W, BK, L, | |
| 1 | | Table Tent | SC, R 10 | |
| 2 | | " " | SC, R 10 | |
| 3 | | K'T. Cabnet | SC, R, 10 4, SC, R, 5,8,9 | |
| 4 | | Microwave | MCU SC, R, | |
| 5 | | Corner Cabnet | R, D, 10,4 SC, R, R-4, | |
| 6 | | K. Table | SC, R, 10, 6 | |
| 7 | | K. Chair | SC, R | |
| 8 | | | SC, R | |
| 9 | | | SC, R | |
| 0 | | K. Chair | SC, R | |
| 1 | | Dish Pack | CP | |
| 2 | | | | |
| 3 | | | | |
| 4 | | | | |
| 5 | | | | |
| 6 | | | | |
| 7 | | | | |
| 8 | | | | |
| 9 | | Dish Pack | CP | |
| 0 | | 4,5 CTN | CP | |
| ITEM NO. | | | | |

"WE HAVE CHECKED ALL THE ITEMS LISTED AND NUMBERED 1 TO ___ INCLUSIVE AND ACKNOWLEDGE THAT THIS IS A TRUE AND COMPLETE LIST OF THE GOODS TENDERED AND OF THE STATE OF THE GOODS RECEIVED"

BEFORE SIGNING CHECK SHIPMENT, COUNT ITEMS AND DESCRIBE LOSS OR DAMAGE IN SPACE ON THE RIGHT ABOVE.

| | TAPE LOT NO. | | TAPE COLOR | |
|---|---|---|---|---|
| | NOS. FROM | | THRU | |

| | CONTRACTOR, CARRIER OR AUTHORIZED AGENT (DRIVER) | DATE | | CONTRACTOR, CARRIER OR AUTHORIZED AGENT (DRIVER) | DATE |
|---|---|---|---|---|---|
| AT ORIGIN | (SIGNATURE) | 1-13-72 | AT DESTI- NATION | (SIGNATURE) | |
| | OWNER OR AUTHORIZED AGENT | DATE | | OWNER OR AUTHORIZED AGENT | DATE |
| | (SIGNATURE) | 1-13-92 | | (SIGNATURE) | |

REORDER MILBIN PRINTING, INC., 135 SCHMITT BLVD., FARMINGDALE, N.Y. 11735

FORM 1190-S REV. '71

73

## Table 8.2 "Extraordinary Value" Sample Inventory

```
(CARRIER NAME)
(Carrier address and telephone No.)
```

ALL ITEMS INCLUDED IN YOUR SHIPMENT THAT ARE CONSIDERED TO BE OF EXTRAORDINARY (UNUSUAL) VALUE MUST BE SPECIFICALLY IDENTIFIED AND THE CARRIER MUST BE ADVISED THAT THEY ARE INCLUDED IN THE SHIPMENT. ITEMS OF EXTRAORDINARY VALUE ARE DEFINED AS THOSE HAVING A VALUE GREATER THAN $100 PER POUND. TYPICAL HOUSEHOLD GOODS ITEMS THAT FREQUENTLY HAVE A VALUE IN EXCESS OF $100 PER POUND PER ARTICLE ARE: CURRENCY, COINS, JEWELRY, PRECIOUS METALS, PRECIOUS OR SEMI-PRECIOUS STONES OR GEMS, GOLD, SILVER OR PLATINUM ARTICLES INCLUDING SILVERWARE AND SERVICE SETS, CHINA SETS, CRYSTAL OR FIGURINES, FUR OR FUR GARMENTS, ANTIQUES, ORIENTAL RUGS OR TAPESTRIES, RARE COLLECTIBLE ITEMS OR OBJECTS OF ART, COMPUTER SOFTWARE PROGRAMS, MANUSCRIPTS OR OTHER RARE DOCUMENTS. OF COURSE, OTHER ITEMS MAY ALSO FALL INTO THIS CATEGORY AND MUST BE IDENTIFIED AS WELL.

**THE PURPOSE OF THIS INVENTORY IS TO ASSIST YOU
IN IDENTIFYING ARTICLES OF EXTRAORDINARY OR UNUSUAL VALUE
IN ORDER THAT THE CARRIER WILL BE AWARE OF THOSE ITEMS
WHICH REQUIRE SPECIAL HANDLING AND PROTECTION
FAILURE TO IDENTIFY SUCH ARTICLES WILL RESULT IN LIMITED CARRIER LIABILITY**

| List No. | Description of Articles Exceeding $100 Per Pound Per Article | List No. | Description of Articles Exceeding $100 Per Pound Per Article |
|---|---|---|---|
| 1. | _____ | 7. | _____ |
| 2. | _____ | 8. | _____ |
| 3. | _____ | 9. | _____ |
| 4. | _____ | 10. | _____ |
| 5. | _____ | 11. | _____ |
| 6. | _____ | 12. | _____ |

OWNER (SHIPPER) AGREES THAT ANY CLAIM FOR LOSS OR DAMAGE MUST BE SUPPORTED BY PROOF OF VALUE AND UNDERSTANDS SETTLEMENT WILL BE BASED UPON THE INFORMATION FURNISHED ON THIS INVENTORY FORM AND THE DECLARATION OF VALUE CONTAINED ON THE ACCOMPANYING BILL OF LADING, THE BILL OF LADING TERMS AND CONDITIONS, THE TARIFF IN EFFECT AT THE TIME OF SHIPMENT, THE HOUSEHOLD GOODS DESCRIPTIVE INVENTORY, AND ALL OTHER PERTINENT INFORMATION AVAILABLE TO THE CARRIER. IF YOU HAVE NOT LISTED ARTICLES HAVING A VALUE IN EXCESS OF $100 PER POUND PER ARTICLE ON THIS INVENTORY, YOUR SIGNATURE BELOW ATTESTS TO THE FACT THAT SUCH ARTICLES ARE NOT INCLUDED IN YOUR SHIPMENT. IF THROUGH INADVERTENCE OR ANY OTHER CAUSE, ITEMS HAVING A VALUE IN EXCESS OF $100 PER POUND PER ARTICLE ARE INCLUDED IN YOUR SHIPMENT AND YOU FAIL TO LIST THOSE ITEMS ON THIS INVENTORY, OR FAIL TO SIGN THIS INVENTORY, YOU EXPRESSLY AGREE THAT THE CARRIER'S LIABILITY FOR LOSS OR DAMAGE TO THOSE ITEMS WILL BE LIMITED TO NO MORE THAN $100 PER POUND PER ARTICLE (BASED UPON THE ACTUAL ARTICLE WEIGHT).

**AT ORIGIN**
I certify the above listed information
to be true, correct and complete.

**CARRIER BILL OF LADING NO.:**

_____

_____     _____
Signature of Shipper          Date
or Shipper's
Representative

Carrier's representative acknowledges
receipt of an executed copy of this
inventory:

_____
Shipment Origin
(City and State)

_____     _____
Signature of                  Date
Carrier's
Representative

latter, mail a photocopy of your inventory sheet directly to the carrier. Don't count on the driver to safeguard all the paperwork. You're paying for the move, the driver isn't.

### Verify Extraordinary Value

Although you don't need to prove the value of ordinary items, you must be able to document the value of something of extraordinary value. Use written appraisals, receipts (if possible), or some sort of photographic evidence.

Appraisals are expensive, but they can be worth it if you lose a valuable item. Professional appraisers charge by flat fee or by the hour—settle all fees before engaging one.

To get the name of an appraiser, ask your banker, insurance agent, or lawyer. Or you can write to the American Society of Appraisers, P.O. Box 17265, Washington, DC 20041, or call 800-272-8258 for a current copy of *Directory of Certified Professional Personal Property Appraisers.*

You should also have clear color photos (or a video) of your valuables. Make a list of these belongings, noting serial numbers or other pertinent information next to each item.

Movers may require that items of extraordinary value be packed only by them, perhaps in custom-made crates. You might consider alternate means of shipping—air, train, bus, post office, or private parcel carrier—for some items.

Although the inventory of your possessions can be tedious and time-consuming (sometimes taking hours), its importance cannot be stressed enough. Make sure that you and the moving company are in agreement. The moving company's investigation must prove the company liable or you won't collect on your claim.

Most companies will try to repair or replace something before reimbursing you for it. This is their option, so be aware of it.

As with other types of valuation, movers will offer different rates as well as deductibles for items of extraordinary value. You'll just have to examine what's offered. Better yet, don't ship anything of extraordinary value on the truck if you can move it yourself. The less you ship, the less your risk. (Check with your airline, shipping line, or the U.S. Customs Service for any restrictions or requirements for international moves.)

## REGULAR INSURANCE

Homeowner's policies may cover goods in transit, and some insurance companies may be willing to add a rider covering them. Consult with your agent. It may be that the rates from your insurance company are better than the rates offered by the mover. Remember, you can collect with less hassle from an insurance company because you don't have to prove liability, just loss.

### Filing a Claim

If you incur a loss or damage on an interstate move, you have nine months from the date of delivery to file a claim, but you should try to file it as soon as possible. If you wait beyond the nine months, the claim will not be considered by the courts. When filing the claim—you can get the proper forms from the mover—it is important to include the following:

• Enough facts to identify the shipment, such as the bill of lading or inventory number, and a description.

• A written assertion that the mover is liable for the alleged loss. For example, it should state something to this effect: "You lost/damaged my *(item)*, and I expect you to repair or replace it."

• A specific dollar amount.

The claim should then be sent directly to the mover, not to the ICC, with return receipt requested.

## GUARANTEED PLEDGE DELAY CLAIM

If you arranged to have your goods picked up or delivered at a specific time and the mover did not meet that schedule through no fault of yours, you can also file a claim for any reasonable expenses you incurred (such as food and lodging) while waiting for the move to be completed. But you must file the claim within the time period specified on the tariff filed by the particular mover. This period is commonly only 30 days.

Your goods are also insured while in storage to the extent you choose, so if they are damaged while in the mover's warehouse, you are also entitled to file a claim.

## ARBITRATION

If you can't resolve a dispute through the claims process, you can take the moving company to court or request that your case go to arbitration. The American Movers Conference, a trade association representing about 1,500 moving companies, has developed an ICC-approved arbitration program for loss or damage claims involving participating member companies in interstate moves.

Either you or the moving company can request arbitration, but both parties must agree in writing to arbitrate. Written arbitration by mail costs you nothing; arbitration with an in-person proceeding costs about $50. The decision of the arbitrator is binding on both parties.

If your mover participates in the arbitration program (you can contact the ICC at any of the addresses listed in the box on page 10 to find out), and your claim involves an interstate move, you can request arbitration by writing to the American Movers Conference, Dispute Settlement Program, 2200 Mill Road, Alexandria, VA 22314. Your letter must be mailed within 60 days after the moving company makes its final offer or denies your claim.

## IMPORTANT POINTS

• What movers provide, in terms of protection for your household goods, is not true insurance but valuation. Companies are potentially liable for the total amount you say your goods are worth. Regular insurance does not consider the question of liability.

• To get anything back on a claim, you have to be able to prove that the loss was the mover's fault. Hence, you should accompany the driver during an inventory to make sure it's accurate, noting exceptions on the inventory form. Watch the unloading of the truck to determine if something has been damaged, in which case you should also note it on the inventory form.

• Take great care to document the worth of extraordinary possessions, getting appraisals, photographic evidence, receipts, and serial numbers.

• Send a copy of the inventory form to the mover, not to the ICC.

• If you want to file a claim, do it quickly even though you officially have nine months to file.

• Filing an international claim will vary from company to company, but it normally must be filed within a month.

• If you incur expenses as a result of movers not meeting their schedule, by all means file a claim. You usually have only a month to file.

• If filing a claim proves unsuccessful, consider arbitration.

# 9

# Countdown to
# Moving Day

As mentioned earlier, it is a good idea to establish a timetable to ensure that your move goes smoothly. The following plan includes suggestions for what you should do as moving day approaches.

If you own a house and are planning to sell it—especially if you will be using the money gained by the sale to purchase your new home—it must be put on the market well in advance of any other arrangement. It would also be a good idea to sit down beforehand and have a discussion with your family about the move; include the children in your talk. As noted in the introduction, a move can be particularly stressful for children.

Owners of condominiums or cooperatives should check with their associations or boards for information on any restrictions that may be imposed on the move. Find out what advance notification is necessary, and get approval, if needed.

If you rent an apartment, check your lease to find out when you are required to notify the

landlord of your move. If there is no formal date, then do so six to eight weeks before the moving date. You want to be able to get back your security deposit, which may mean that you have to allow enough time to fix any damage to the apartment. Damage costs will otherwise be deducted from the security deposit.

The timetable below is not meant to be cast in stone—you may have priorities that prevent you from following it exactly—but the point is that you should have some schedule. To leave everything until the last minute will only create chaos.

## SIX TO EIGHT WEEKS
## BEFORE THE MOVE

• Shop around for a mover, asking friends and checking other sources for names. Once you have compiled a list, check them out (see chapter 1).

• Determine what extra charges (to the extent possible) are to be expected at the origin and destination. These include elevator charges, stair carry charges, etc. This information will help the mover prepare an accurate estimate.

• Schedule time to have movers come in and give estimates.

• Plan a garage sale to reduce the number of items you will be taking with you. Remember, you want the estimates to be based only on what is to be shipped. Make a floor plan of your new home, complete with space measurements, to help you determine what to keep and what to dispose of. (For example, some of your furniture may not fit into your new home.)

• Talk with your homeowner's insurance agent about coverage for your household goods while they are in transit.

• If your employer is going to pay for part or all of the move, make sure the mover gets paid on time.

• If you are going to ship items of extraordinary value, look to see if you have sales slips for them. Take photos or videos of the items, and make contact with professional appraisers to get documentation as to their worth.

• Check into alternate shipping methods that may save you money.

• If you are going to move yourself, start collecting boxes and other moving materials.

• If you are traveling to your destination by air, train, or bus, start shopping around for the best deal.

• Notify the post office of your new address, and obtain change-of-address cards.

• If you are going to a new state, write to the state department of motor vehicles and find out how to apply for a license. Your current license may be transferable. If you are moving out of the United States, ask the consulate of the country you're moving to about how to obtain a driver's license.

• Start gathering important documents.

• Select a new school for your children, and obtain copies of school transcripts. If possible, start the process of transferring school records sooner than six to eight weeks before the move.

• Clear up any outstanding tax bills.

• Start closing out charge accounts that will not be needed in your new location.

• Start thinking about applying for credit in your new location.

• Contact your insurance agents and ask how you can transfer your insurance (home, auto, boat) so that the protection is continuous.

• Talk with your banker about how to transfer money from savings or checking accounts, or the contents of safe-deposit boxes, to a new bank or banks (but don't make arrangements to do so until about a week before you move). Perhaps your banker has other recommendations. It's a good idea to open an account at your destination before you arrive so you don't have to deal with the hassle of trying to cash out-of-state (or out-of-country) checks.

• Ask your dentist and doctor to prepare your medical records for transfer to your new community. If possible, your doctor and dentist should recommend someone at your new location.

• Contact the utility companies at your new location, and tell them the date you'd like services started.

• Contact everyone in your present or future location who might need to know about the move: school administrator, attorney, broker, pharmacist, telephone company, state or federal tax agencies, library, motor vehicle department, draft board, Social Security Administration, Department of Veterans Affairs, businesses where you have accounts (emergency road service, bakery, cleaner, dairy, department stores, diaper service, finance companies, laundry, service stations, fuel company, etc.).

• If you have any borrowed items, return them. Also, get back items you may have loaned out.

• Write for letters of reference if you will need them to find work at your new location.

• If your old home is not yet sold, make all necessary repairs and cosmetic changes (paint, wallpaper, cleaning) to make it more sellable.

• Get a copy of the IRS publications relevant to moving.

## FOUR WEEKS BEFORE THE MOVE

• Pick the moving company you're going to use.

• Start packing seldom-used items. For example, if you're moving during the summer, pack heavy blankets. You may pack other items, but take care not to pack something that you may have to use before or during the move.

• If you will be taking pets, start making inquiries concerning how to move them. Determine what a particular airline's requirements may be for shipping animals.

• If you will need a storage facility, think about which one you're going to use.

• Make final decisions on what you are taking and what you are leaving. Alert your moving company representative of any late changes to see if anything will impact on the company's bid.

• If you want to join a club or need a license or permit for something at your new location, apply during this period to avoid a long wait when you get there.

• Write to the chamber of commerce (or similar agency) in your new location and ask for literature that will familiarize you with the area. Remember, many movers have get-acquainted literature available.

## TWO WEEKS BEFORE THE MOVE

• Continue to pack whatever you can. You may want to designate a couple of empty closets as temporary holding places.

• Send out rugs and drapes to be cleaned as needed. When they return, keep protective wrappings in place so you can ship the rugs and drapes properly.

• Call utility companies and tell them when to turn off your service.

• Make necessary arrangements for shipping houseplants.

• Before packing your address book, make a list of the numbers you may need to call in the meantime. (Remember to take the telephone directory, too.)

• Arrange for servicing of appliances if you are having them moved by specialists.

• Arrange to have grandfather clocks, pool tables, chandeliers, television antennas, and any other special items readied for shipment.

• Have your car fully serviced. (It's better to get it done by a trustworthy mechanic who knows your car.)

• Make arrangements to have cars, boats, or trailers shipped.

• Mail change-of-address cards.

• Call the moving company to confirm details of the move. Remember to keep the lines of communication open.

• Confirm whatever travel plans you have made.

• Advertise another garage sale if the first one was not very successful.

• If you're going to have a farewell party, notify friends and neighbors a week before the date. When you have the party, use paper plates and plastic cups.

## ONE WEEK BEFORE THE MOVE

• Double-check that the movers have your complete information, such as your destination address and your itinerary en route, just in case they need to get in touch with you while you travel.

• Drain fuel and oil from your lawn mower, snowblower, or similar equipment.

• Start to pack suitcases.

• Check your home for remaining items you may want to discard.

• Make sure you have gathered all the documents you want to take with you.

• Empty the barbecue propane tank (check with propane company on how to do this), clean the grill, and pack loose parts.

• If necessary, make arrangements to have a baby-sitter watch your children on the day you must pack. Then you can concentrate on your moving chores.

• If you are due a refund for security deposits on utilities, rent, phone, and the like, alert parties of your new address. If you can, pick the money up or have it sent to you before you move.

• Sometime during the week, drop off boxes to be shipped from the post office, United Parcel Service, or other shipper (exactly when you should do this depends on the shipper's estimate of the boxes' arrival date and when you're going to need the articles).

• If your employer is paying for the move, check with the mover to make sure that your employer's credit has been approved (the mover will conduct an investigation). Otherwise, you may have to pay for the shipment before it is unloaded.

• Close bank accounts, and make arrangements to transfer money and contents of safe-deposit boxes. Buy traveler's checks and purchase a certified bank check or money order to pay the mover.

• Gather tools and other items in your car to serve as an emergency travel kit.

• Cancel newspaper delivery.

• Make final arrangements for moving pets.

• Pay any outstanding fines.

• Dispose of houseplants that you're not shipping.

• Start throwing out or consuming food that you're not taking with you.

• Arrange to have any remaining items dry-cleaned, and launder items as needed.

## Items to Take with You

The following is a checklist of items that you should consider taking with you instead of loading onto the mover's truck.

**Car-Related Items**
• Tools
• Aerosol tire inflator
• Jack and lug wrench
• Fire extinguisher
• Flashlight
• Road maps and compass
• Driver's license
• Car registration
• Auto insurance cards
• Duplicate keys
• Litter basket

**Valuables**
• Jewelry
• Furs
• Silverware
• Stamp or coin collections
• Photos, slides, home videos
• Any other items of extraordinary value you can fit into the car

**Important Documents**
• Automobile titles
• School records
• Dental and medical records
• Insurance policies
• Other records (medical, employment, tax)

**Miscellaneous**
• Credit cards
• Sunglasses
• Toys
• Baby's changing and feeding items
• Water for pets and people
• Paper towels
• Premoistened towelettes for cleaning
• Pillows and blankets
• Pet food and pet dishes
• Camera, film
• List of important telephone numbers

• Pack pictures, paintings, mirrors, and other items hanging on the walls.

• Pack jewelry and other valuables you want to take with you.

## ONE OR TWO DAYS BEFORE THE MOVE

• If your home will be vacant for a while after you move, alert police and neighbors to this.

• Call utility companies to confirm service shutoff.

• Confirm any reservations you've made—rental car, motels, etc.

• If you're having the contents of your home professionally packed, the packers will arrive one or two days before the move.

• Dispose of or give away any remaining items you don't need. (Don't forget the contents of drawers.)

• If you have opted for a nonbinding estimate and want to witness the weighing of your goods, call the moving company for information on where the weighings will take place.

• Confirm the arrangements for a baby-sitter you may have hired.

• All packing should be done or nearly completed, but double-check boxes for complete labeling ("Fragile," "This Side Up," "Load Last," etc.).

• Begin cleaning the house.

• Start loading the car.

• Defrost the refrigerator, cleaning as needed. For a clean smell, place an open box of baking soda inside when you're finished.

• If you need a hired car to take you to the airport, pier, railroad, or bus, arrange for the pickup.

• If you're getting a ride from a friend or neighbor to an airport or train station, confirm arrangements.

• Write out your new address on a slip of paper and tape it in a prominent location in the house. The new occupant may need to contact you, or perhaps forward mail to you.

• Retrieve any items from the laundry, dry cleaner, or other service. If you've had rugs or drapes cleaned, don't forget to retrieve them.

• Take apart large furniture pieces as needed.

• To make it easy for the movers, give the driver a map of the area you are moving to. Indicate the destination, marked off clearly on the map.

# 10

# Moving Day

IF you've prepared properly and there are no unusual circumstances (bad weather, illness, transportation delays, etc.), the day of the move should go relatively smoothly. You'll then be free to concentrate on the things that you still have to do.

## LAST-MINUTE CHORES

A variety of household chores and other details will likely need to be done to ensure a problem-free move for everyone. They include the following:

• Double-check what you're taking with you.
• Pack any food or drinks you want to carry along.
• Put out the garbage. If pickup is not scheduled for a few days, ask neighbors if you can put your garbage in their containers. Otherwise, dogs, cats, or birds may scatter the garbage all over the place.

• Remove bedclothes.
• Take apart a water bed.
• Lock all doors and windows.
• Vacuum each room as it is emptied.
• Return keys to your landlord, rental agent, etc.

*Tip:* It's not a good idea to use the television on moving day. Internal parts can crack if moved when hot.

## BILL OF LADING

When the movers arrive, they will have the previously mentioned bill of lading ready for your signature. This is a crucial document, literally the contract between you and the mover. Compare the information on it—prices, services, etc.—with what's on the order for service (you should have a clear copy). The information should be identical.

You will be required to sign the document,

# Table 10.1 Bill of Lading

| 1. ALL CHARGES TO BE PAID IN CASH, POSTAL MONEY ORDER OR CASHIER'S CHECK PAYABLE TO ATLAS VAN LINES BEFORE PROPERTY IS RELINQUISHED BY CARRIER UNLESS OTHERWISE STATED. ON EMPLOYER PAID MOVES, SHIPPER IS LIABLE FOR ALL CARRIER CHARGES IF EMPLOYER FAILS TO MAKE PAYMENT AS PROMISED. | 2. ALL TERMS PRINTED OR STAMPED HEREON OR ON THE REVERSE SIDE HEREOF. | 3. RATES, RULES AND REGULATIONS IN TARIFF __400H__ SEC. __3__ |

SHIPPER REQUESTS    REWEIGH ☐    NOTIFICATION OF ACTUAL WEIGHT & CHARGES  ☐ NO  ☒ YES

AGREED PICKUP PERIOD __1/25/93__  AGREED DEL. PERIOD __1/29-2/9__

TO _____   TEL. _____
IN CASE OF DELAY NOTIFY __CERTIFIED VAN__  TEL. __800/645-7210__

ADDRESS _____   ADDRESS __KATHY ESSIG__

UNLESS THE SHIPPER EXPRESSLY RELEASES THE SHIPMENT TO A VALUE OF 60 CENTS PER POUND PER ARTICLE, THE CARRIER'S MAXIMUM LIABILITY FOR LOSS AND DAMAGE SHALL BE EITHER THE LUMP SUM VALUE DECLARED BY THE SHIPPER OR AN AMOUNT EQUAL TO $1.25 FOR EACH POUND OF RATED WEIGHT IN THE SHIPMENT, WHICHEVER IS GREATER.

The shipment will move subject to the rules and conditions of the carrier's tariff. Shipper hereby releases the entire shipment to a value not exceeding

(1) I hereby release this shipment at Atlas legal liability of $.60 per pound per article.

_____ (Shipper or Representative) _____ (Date)

(2) I hereby release this shipment to Atlas with maximum carrier's liability at $_____ (Insert amount per pound or lump sum value). The amount inserted must be a minimum of $1.25 per pound times the actual weight.

_____ (Shipper or Representative) _____ (Date)

### FULL VALUE PROTECTION
(3) By signature below, the shipper elects this protection option excluding the released rate and declared value options (by so doing shipper accepts to the terms of Full Value Protection Plan as provided in carrier's tariffs). Otherwise the shipment is released as provided in MC-505 elsewhere declared herein.

I declare this shipment is to be released with Full Value Protection

In the amount of $_____ This amount must be the sum indicated in the tariff item based on the full value option selected, but not less than $3.50 per lb. times the actual weight of the shipment subject to a $10,000.00 minimum released value per shipment.

#### FVP DEDUCTIBLE SELECTION
OPTION A ☐ NO DEDUCTIBLE    OPTION B ☐ $250 DEDUCTIBLE    OPTION C ☐ $500 DEDUCTIBLE

_____ (Shipper or Representative) _____ (Date)

NOTICE:
THE SHIPPER SIGNING THIS CONTRACT MUST INSERT HIS OWN SIGNATURE IN ONE OF THE SPACES ABOVE, OTHERWISE THE SHIPMENT WILL BE DEEMED RELEASED AT A MAXIMUM VALUE EQUAL TO $1.25 TIMES THE ACTUAL WEIGHT OF THE SHIPMENT IN POUNDS.

Provided that: Where the shipper is the employer of the actual owner of the household goods being transported and is responsible for all transportation charges in connection with such a move, the shipper may instruct the motor carrier to release the shipment to a value of 60 cents per pound per article, a declared value or full value protection (a) by specification made on a purchase order, or (b) by issuing, in advance of shipment date, appropriate letters of instruction to the carrier. In such instances, the motor carrier must incorporate the instruction by reference to the document stated above in the bill of lading in lieu of the personal signature and handwritten statement relating to released rates.

### IMPORTANT
If a review and comparison of items to be shipped and services rendered reflect that items, services or combinations thereof were added to the shipment after the survey, the carrier reserves the right upon notification to the shipper to void Binding Cost of Service Estimate and/or Order for Service. Review and comparison of items and services by carrier may not be completed on this shipment until after loading. If the Binding Cost of Service Estimate and/or Order for Service are voided by the carrier, transportation charges shall be based on actual weight and actual services rendered payable in full on or before delivery.

ATLAS VAN LINES, INC. AND THE ABOVE NAMED SHIPPER AGREE THAT ATLAS VAN LINES, INC., THE CARRIER, SHALL TRANSPORT THE GOODS AND EFFECTS TENDERED BY THE SHIPPER.

SIGNED X _____ (SHIPPER) _____ DATE
CARRIER _____
DRIVER _____ ATLAS VAN LINES, INC.

#### AGENT SERVICE DATA

| | Agent's No. |
|---|---|
| AUTHORIZATION NO. _____ | |
| BOOKED BY __CERTIFIED__ | 598 |
| ORIGIN AGENT __CERTIFIED__ | 598 |
| PACKED BY __ABC__ | 20 |
| DATE LOADED AT RES. __1/25/93__ | 20 |
| BY __ABCq__ | 20 |
| DATE LOADED AT WHSE. _____ | |
| BY _____ | |
| HAULER 1 __Wiseman__   AVL TRAILER # | |
| FROM __Org__   TO __Dest__ | 20 |
| HAULER 2   AVL TRAILER # | |
| FROM _____ TO _____ | |
| DATE DELIVERED _____ | 20 |

#### ON ARRIVAL CONTACT
DEST. AGENT __EDS M&S__   823
AND __MARTY DOLAN__
SIT AUTH. AT _____
BY _____ PER _____

Extraordinary (Unusual) Value Article Declaration I acknowledge that I have prepared and retained a copy of the "Inventory of Items Valued in Excess of $100 Per Pound Per Article" that are included in my shipment and that I have given a copy of this inventory to the carrier's representative. I also acknowledge that the carrier's liability for loss or damage to any article valued in excess of $100 per pound will be limited to $100 per pound for each pound of such lost or damaged article (based on actual article weight), not to exceed the declared value of the entire shipment, unless I have specifically identified such articles for which a claim for loss or damage is made on the attached inventory.

Shipper _____
Date _____ I decline (_____)  SIGNED X _____

### SPECIAL SERVICES ORDERED

☐ EXPEDITED SERVICE ORDERED BY _____
☐ SHIPPER DELIVER ON OR BEFORE _____
☐ SHIPMENT COMPLETELY OCCUPIED A _____ CU. FT. VEHICLE
☐ EXCLUSIVE USE OF A _____ CU. FT. VEHICLE ORDERED
☐ SPACE RESERVATION _____ CU. FT. ORDERED
☐ SELECTIVE DELIVERY DATE SERVICE ORDERED BY SHIPPER
  DELIVER ON OR BEFORE _____

| | WEIGHT |
|---|---|
| GROSS | 45,600 |
| TARE | 39,340 |
| NET | 6,260 |
| GROSS | |
| TARE | |
| NET | |

| CODE # | SERVICES | RATE | CHARGE |
|---|---|---|---|
| | TRANSPORTATION MILES __2839__   BCS WEIGHT | | |
| 4000 | LB. BASE TRANSPORTATION CHARGE $ __4,604.00__ | | |
| 2260 | LBS. @ __93.73__/CWT  $ __2,118.29__ | | 6,722.29 |
| | L/H FACTOR | | |
| | INSURANCE SURCHARGE | | 268.89 |
| | SMALL SHIPMENT CHARGE | | |
| 20 | ADD TRANS.   ORIG. 3.25   DEST. .90 | 4.15 | 259.79 |
| | CONTAINERS __34.90__ PACKING __36.40__ | | 71.30 |
| | UNPACKING __14.40__ | | 14.40 |
| 20 | __Bulky Article    Auto__ | 113.05 | 113.05 |
| | APPLIANCE SERVICES { ORIGIN DUE | | |
| | { DEST. DUE | | |
| | BINDING COST OF SERVICE CONTAINERS, PACKING AND UNPACKING | | |
| | OTHER BCS SERVICES | | |
| | TOTAL BCS CHARGES | | |
| | PIANO HANDLING | | |
| | FLIGHT   NO | | |
| | ELEVATOR | | |
| | EXCESSIVE DISTANCE CARRY  Feet | | |
| | EXTRA LABOR  Men    Man Hrs. | | |
| | EXTRA PICKUPS OR DELIVERIES _____ LBS. | | |
| | AT | | |
| | VALUATION $ __9,000.00__   .50 Per $100.00 | | 45.00 |
| | F.V.P. Wt.   Per tariff $ | | |
| | SIT 1ST DAY   WEIGHT | | |
| | FROM   TO   2nd & Add Days   @ | | |
| | WAREHOUSE HANDLING | | |
| | CARTAGE TO WHSE.   FROM WHSE.   CHARGE $ | | |
| | MI.   /CWT  $ | | |
| | SIT VALUATION | | |
| | SIT VALUATION/SUM   1st. Mo.   2nd. Mo. | | |
| | BLD __45__ % of $ __7,449.72__ | | 3,352.37 |
| | ☐ CHGE  ☐ PPD  ☒ COD  ☐ GBL  ☐ CREDIT CARD   TOTAL CHARGES | | 4,142.35 |
| | PREPAYMENT COLLECTED BY | | |
| | ESTIMATED CHARGES $ __4,346.1/__  110% COLLECTION OPTION $ __4,780.78__ | | |
| | BALANCE DUE COLLECTED BY | | |

INVOICING CONTRACT/P.O./G.B.L. -NO. __145BLD__
BILL CHARGES TO _____
Re appropriate tariff subject to minimum weight of 500 lbs. or 1000 lbs. __1000__ or _____ Min Charges
STREET _____
CITY, STATE _____
ATTN. _____

REC'D FOR STORAGE _____ (WAREHOUSE)
BY _____ (WAREHOUSEMAN'S SIGNATURE) _____ PER _____ DATE

DELIVERY ACKNOWLEDGMENT: SHIPMENT WAS RECEIVED IN GOOD CONDITION EXCEPT AS NOTED ON INVENTORY AND SERVICES ORDERED WERE PERFORMED.

SIGNED X _____ DATE _____

DC-202006
Rev. 6/91

and so will the driver. But don't sign it until you're sure everything is as it should be. This may require some scrutiny, but it is well worth the time taken. Get a legible copy. If this document or any other isn't legible, it's of no value.

# INVENTORY

Taking inventory is another moving-day procedure. When the movers start preparing your goods for shipment, they will tag or otherwise label all the goods with a number, and will check them off their inventory sheet. They will also note the condition of the shipment. Again, verify what they indicate, and object to any information you disagree with.

# WEIGHING THE SHIPMENT

If the mover's fee is based on the weight of the shipment, the mover is required to weigh the shipment. If it weighs less than 1,000 pounds, the mover can do this using a warehouse platform scale. Otherwise, either *origin* or *destination* weighing is used (see chapter 2 for more information on weighing). In essence, tare weight (the empty truck) is subtracted from gross weight (the truck with all your belongings in it) to yield net weight, which is what you will be charged for.

## Observe Weighings

You have the right—a right you should definitely exercise—to witness any and all weighings. To initiate this, indicate your intentions when you sign the order for service. Then the company can alert you when and where the shipment is to be weighed and allow you time to get to the location.

Every time the truck is weighed, the mover is required to obtain a weight ticket showing the date and place of weighing. ICC rules also dictate that the ticket indicate your name and shipment number on it, along with the identification number of the truck. Additionally, the ticket must be signed by the person at the weigh station who recorded the weight. If the same scale is used to record both gross and tare weights, the same ticket may be used.

## Protect Against Rip-offs

The chief industry rip-off is called "weight bumping." This is simply making a shipment appear to weigh more than it does. This is the reason people use binding estimates. Weight bumping is not a minor crime. If the mover gets caught, the statutory penalty is a fine of at least $1,000, up to a maximum of $10,000, and two years in jail.

Here are a few ways movers get away with weight bumping:

• Movers can improperly adjust weight or weight tickets. They can make the tare weight lower by perhaps not loading all moving equipment on the truck. After they weigh the truck, then they load up their equipment, go to your house, load your shipment, and reweigh the truck. Thus, you end up paying for all the equipment that was not part of the original weighing.

• Companies can weigh the truck with the fuel tanks empty.

• Companies can load numerous heavy items such as bricks, steel plates, or the like for a heavier gross weight.

## Disagreeing with Weight

If you think the weight of your goods is excessive, you have the right to get a free reweighing before unloading. If the reweigh is different from the first weigh, the carrier must refigure the charges and reduce your bill accordingly.

Of course, the reweigh may not necessarily go in your favor, and if it doesn't, you must pay the higher charges. However, there is a way to calculate the shipment weight to determine if it's in your best interest to reweigh.

First, count the number of items in your shipment. (Usually there will be 30 to 40 items per inventory page.) If a car is part of the shipment, subtract its weight as listed on the car title or license from the total weight of the shipment quoted by the mover. Then divide the number of items you counted into the total weight. If the number you get is between 35 and 45, it's unlikely that a reweigh will be in your best interest. According to the ICC, most items weigh an average of 40 pounds. If you are shipping heavy tools, boxes of books, and similarly weighty items, the average may be 45 pounds or more.

## PAYING THE BILL

Payment of the transportation charges (basic charges for loading and unloading) is required before the shipment will be unloaded. This bill is submitted to you at the destination. Normally, movers will simply use a copy of the bill of lading as a freight bill, but some movers use entirely different documents.

Unless the bill is for a binding estimate, it must specifically identify each service performed, the rate or unit price for each service, and the total charges. You should not accept a bill that doesn't contain this information; if you do, you don't really know what you're paying for.

If you have shipped your goods under a nonbinding estimate and the final charges prove to be more than the estimate (more than 110 percent), full payment is not required on delivery day, as mentioned previously. Movers normally require payment in the form of a money order, bank draft, or certified check but will not accept a personal check unless this has been previously approved. Some movers will allow you to pay by credit card, but it's not a good idea to

assume this, even if you have a nationally accepted card. Finally, if you don't pay at all, movers have the right to keep your goods in storage until you pay.

## TWO-TRUCK SHIPMENT

Although movers strive to ship all goods on one truck, it sometimes becomes necessary to use two trucks. This is not uncommon—for example, when a car has to be shipped. Household goods will travel on one truck, and the car will travel on another truck designed for transporting automobiles.

If the shipment requires two trucks, you are usually not required to pay for the shipment until everything has been delivered. On the other hand, some movers require payment for any portion that is delivered. This is another detail to check out when you are arranging for a move.

## BILLING ERRORS

If there is an error on the bill, attempt to correct it immediately with the driver, the destination agent, or someone at the main office (you can call the mover's toll-free number). If you discover an error after the delivery of the goods, write to the mover and describe the error. Movers usually double-check bills themselves to ensure that charges are accurate. If they find you were overcharged, they will notify you and issue a refund. If undercharged, you will be billed for additional charges.

## UNLOADING

It is wise to be present for the unloading of your goods, but it is generally not a good idea to actually participate unless you need a particular item right away. Otherwise, your involvement should be limited to giving the movers directions. Ideally, one person can stay outside and instruct the movers where to put items and another person inside can make sure they put them there.

## WATCH FOR DAMAGE

Remember, it is important to watch for damage and note it immediately on the inventory form when it occurs. If a box is dented or damaged, open it in the presence of the movers and note the nature of the damage. If a representative is not available, leave the box as is until someone from the moving company can inspect it.

If you have paid the movers to unpack, they should do this after all of the items have been placed in their respective rooms. They are required to place items where they belong (or approximately where they belong).

## FIRST DAYS

As you settle into your new home, there are a few things you can do to make the adjustment period smoother. These include the following:

• Get the kitchen, bath, and bedrooms in order.

• Place houseplants in a bright room but out of direct sunlight for a couple of days. Water only if necessary. This will ease the plants' transition to the new environment.

• Take the kids for a walk or drive in the neighborhood.

• Introduce yourself to the neighbors. They'll be able to answer questions on a wide variety of subjects. In addition, your gesture could alleviate any anxiety your neighbors have about you.

• Wait a couple of weeks before hanging pictures. You may not like the original furniture arrangement, and this of course will affect picture placement.

## IMPORTANT POINTS

• Compare the information on the bill of lading with the information that's on the order for service. They should be the same. Remember, the bill of lading is the real contract for the move.

• If you have a nonbinding estimate, observe the weighing of your goods.

• Witness the unloading of your goods at the destination. If you see that something has been damaged, note it immediately on the inventory form (your copy as well as the mover's copy).

# Appendix A

## STATE MOVING REGULATORS

State regulation of the moving industry is a hodgepodge affair, to say the least. It is essential to check with the controlling body, if any, to get descriptive literature relevant to your move, and to see if the mover is licensed and insured. (The ICC's Office of Compliance and Consumer Assistance is located in Room 4133, ICC Building, 12th Street and Constitution Avenue NW, Washington, DC 20423.) Once you have this information in hand, you can do a better job of selecting a mover and protecting yourself.

The following is a list of states that at least have a regulatory body in place. (Alaska, Arizona, Colorado, Delaware, Hawaii, Maine, New Mexico, and Vermont are not regulated.)

### Alabama
Alabama Public Service Commission
Transportation Division/Legal Division
State Office Building
P.O. Box 991
Montgomery, AL 36101-0991
(205) 261-5200

### Arkansas
Arkansas State Highway and Transportation
  Department
P.O. Box 2261
Little Rock, AR 72203
(501) 371-1341

### California
California Public Utilities Commission
505 Van Ness Avenue
San Francisco, CA 94102
(415) 557-1487

### Connecticut
Connecticut Department of Transportation
Bureau of Public Transportation
375 Willard Avenue
P.O. Box 11-998
Newington, CT 06111-0998
(203) 566-4010

## Florida
Florida Transportation Department
605 Suwannee Street
Tallahassee, FL 32399

## Georgia
Georgia Public Service Commission
1007 Virginia Avenue
Suite 310
Hapeville, GA 30354
(404) 559-6602

## Idaho
Idaho Transportation Department
3311 West State Street
P.O. Box 7129
Boise, ID 83707

## Illinois
Illinois Commerce Commission
Transportation Division
527 East Capitol Avenue
Springfield, IL 62706
(217) 782-4654

## Indiana
Indiana Department of Revenue
Room N240
100 North Senate Avenue
Indianapolis, IN 46204
(317) 232-6201

## Iowa
Iowa Department of Transportation
Office of Motor Carrier Services
5238 Northwest 2nd Avenue
Des Moines, IA 50313
(515) 281-5664

## Kansas
Kansas Corporation Commission
1500 Southwest Arrowhead Road
Topeka, KS 66604-4027
(913) 296-3000

## Kentucky
Kentucky Division of Motor Carriers
P.O. Box 2007
Frankfort, KY 40602
(502) 564-4540

## Louisiana
Louisiana Public Service Commission
P.O. Box 91154
Baton Rouge, LA 70821
(504) 342-4439

## Maryland
Maryland Transportation Department
P.O. Box 8755
BWI Airport, MD 21240

## Massachusetts
Massachusetts Department of Public Utilities
Transportation Division
Room 1203
100 Cambridge Street
Boston, MA 02202
(617) 727-3559

## Michigan
Michigan Public Service Commission
Motor Carrier Division
Authorities Section
1048 Pierpont, Suite 4
Lansing, MI 48909
(517) 334-6389

## Minnesota
Minnesota Office of Motor Carrier Safety and
    Compliance
152 Livestock Exchange Building
100 Stockyards Road
South St. Paul, MN 55075
(612) 961-5439

## Mississippi
Mississippi Public Service Commission
P.O. Box 1174
Jackson, MS 39215-1174
(601) 961-5439

## Missouri
Missouri Division of Transportation
P.O. Box 1216
301 West High Street, HST Building
Jefferson City, MO 65102
(314) 751-7100

## Montana
Montana Public Service Commission
1701 Prospect Avenue
Helena, MT 59601
(406) 444-6198

## Nebraska
Nebraska Public Service Commission
P.O. Box 94927
300 The Atrium
1200 North Street
Lincoln, NE 68509-4927
(402) 471-3101

## Nevada
Public Service of Nevada
727 Fairview Drive
Carson City, NV 89710
(702) 687-6006

## New Hampshire
New Hampshire Department of Safety
Division of Motor Vehicles
Common Carriers Bureau
10 Hazen Drive
Concord, NH 03305

## New Jersey
New Jersey State Board of Public Movers and
   Warehousemen
124 Halsey Street
Newark, NJ 07102
(201) 504-6475

## New York
New York State Department of Transportation
Carrier Certification & Compliance Bureau
Bldg. 7A, Room 405
1220 Washington Avenue
Albany, NY 12232
(518) 457-6503

## North Carolina
North Carolina Utilities Commission
Transportation Division
P.O. Box 29510
Raleigh, NC 27626
(919) 733-4035

## North Dakota
Transportation Division
Public Service Commission
State of North Dakota
State Capitol
Bismarck, ND 58505
(701) 224-2400

## Ohio
Public Utilities Commission of Ohio
Transportation Department
180 West Broad Street
Columbus, OH 43266-0573
(614) 466-3392

## Oklahoma
Transportation Division
Oklahoma Corporation Commission
Jim Thorpe Building
Oklahoma City, OK 73105
(405) 521-2251

## Oregon
Oregon Public Utility Commission
350 Winter Street NE
Salem, OR 97301
(503) 378-6664

## Pennsylvania
Bureau of Transportation
Pennsylvania Public Utilities Commission
P.O. Box 3265
Harrisburg, PA 17120
(717) 787-2154

## Rhode Island
Rhode Island Public Utilities Commission
Motor Carrier Section
100 Orange Street
Providence, RI 02903
(401) 277-3500

**South Carolina**
South Carolina Public Service Commission
Transportation Division
P.O. Drawer 11649
Columbia, SC 29211
(803) 737-5178

**South Dakota**
South Dakota Public Utilities Commission
Transportation Division
State Capitol Building
Pierre, SD 57501
(605) 773-3201

**Tennessee**
Tennessee Public Service Commission
Transportation Division
460 James Robertson Parkway
Nashville, TN 37243-0505
(615) 741-2974

**Texas**
Railroad Corporation of Texas
Transportation Division
Capitol Station
P.O. Box 12967
Austin, TX 78711
(512) 463-7122

**Utah**
State of Utah Department of Commerce
Division of Public Utilities
Motor Carrier Section
160 East 300 South
P.O. Box 45807
Salt Lake City, UT 84145-0807
(801) 530-6662

**Virginia**
State Corporation Commission
Motor Carrier Division
P.O. Box 1419
Richmond, VA 23211
(804) 786-2096

**Washington**
Washington Utilities and Transportation
   Commission
1300 South Evergreen Park Drive SW
P.O. Box 9022
Olympia, WA 98504-9022
(206) 753-3111

**West Virginia**
West Virginia Public Service Commission
201 Brooks Street
P.O. Box 812
Charleston, WV 25323
(304) 340-0320

**Wisconsin**
Wisconsin Transportation Bureau
Motor Carrier Bureau
Room 403
212 East Washington Street
Madison, WI 53708-8968
(608) 266-2671

**Wyoming**
Regulatory Program
Wyoming Department of Transportation
5300 Bishop Boulevard
P.O. Box 1708
Cheyenne, WY 82002-9019
(307) 777-7423

# Appendix B

## ADDRESSES OF MOVING COMPANIES

The following are the corporate headquarters of the moving companies that made at least 100 moves in 1991:

### California
Global Van Lines
2301 North Glassell Street
Orange, CA 92665

Starving Students, Inc.
8525 West Pico Boulevard
Los Angeles, CA 90035

### Colorado
Apaca Van Lines, Inc.
5051 East 50th Avenue
Denver, CO 80216

### Florida
Terminal Van Lines, Inc.
12425 U.S. 19 North
Clearwater, FL 34624

Fogarty Van Lines, Inc.
1103 Cumberland Avenue
P.O. Box 3402
Tampa, FL 33601

### Georgia
Burnham Service Co., Inc.
P.O. Box 7966
Columbus, GA 31908

### Illinois
Allied Van Lines
500 Park Place
Naperville, IL 60863

All Points Vans, Inc.
1400 Chase Avenue
Elk Grove, IL 60007

Bekins Van Lines
330 South Mannheim Road
Hillside, IL 60162

Mid-West Moving and Storage Inc.
3048 North Lake Terrace
Glenview, IL 60025

National Van Lines, Inc.
2800 Roosevelt Road
Broadview, IL 60153

New World Lines, Inc.
5875 North Rogers
Chicago, IL 60646

North Shore Movers, Inc.
600 Waukegan Road
P.O. Box 189
Northbrook, IL 60065

## Indiana
American Red Ball Transit
P.O. Box 1127
1335 Sadlier Circle, East Drive
Indianapolis, IN 46206

Atlas Van Lines
P.O. Box 509
1212 St. George Road
Evansville, IN 47703

Mayflower Transit, Inc.
P.O. Box 107
Indianapolis, IN 46206

North American Van Lines
5001 U.S. Highway 30 West
Fort Wayne, IN 46818

Wheaton Van Lines, Inc.
8010 Castleton Road
P.O. Box 50800
Indianapolis, IN 46250

## Louisiana
Security Van Lines, Inc.
P.O. Box 830
Kenner, LA 70063

## Maryland
Mercury Van Lines, Inc.
18930 Woodfield Road
Gaithersburg, MD 20879

## Massachusetts
F. L. Castine, Inc.
1235 Chestnut Street
Athol, MA 01331

Clark & Reid Company, Inc.
P.O. Box 426
Meadow Road
Burlington, MA 01803

J. McCabe & Son, Inc.
152 Tremont Street
Melrose, MA 02176

## Michigan
Corrigan Moving & Storage Co.
2000 Westwood
Dearborn, MI 48124

Stevens Van Lines
P.O. Box 3276
527 Morley Drive
Saginaw, MI 48605

## Mississippi
Morgan Van Lines
P.O. Box 419
Booneville, MS 38829

## Missouri
Carlyle Van Lines
600 North Main Street
P.O. Box 47
Warrensburg, MO 64093

Stieferman Brothers Van & Storage Co.
10899 Indian Head Industrial
St. Louis, MO 63132

United Van Lines
1 United Drive
Fenton, MO 63206

Von Der Ahe Van Lines, Inc.
600 Rudder Road
Fenton, MO 63206

**Nebraska**
Andrews Van Lines
7th and Park Avenue
P.O. Box 1609
Norfolk, NE 68702

**New Hampshire**
McGlaughlin Transportation Systems, Inc.
20 Progress Avenue
Nashua, NH 03062

**New Jersey**
Bohren's Moving & Storage, Inc.
755 Alexander Road
Princeton, NJ 08540

Frank Malatesta, Inc.
61 Iowa Avenue
Paterson, NJ 07503

**New York**
A-1 Family Moving & Storage, Inc.
8 Picone Boulevard
Farmingdale, NY 11735

All States Transfer & Storage, Inc.
79-17 Albion Avenue
Elmhurst, NY 11373

Cook Moving Systems, Inc.
1845 Dale Road
Buffalo, NY 14225

CTC Van Lines, Inc.
470 Pulaski Street
Brooklyn, NY 11221

P. J. Garvey Carting & Storage, Inc.
465 Cornwall Avenue
Buffalo, NY 14215

Verity Van Lines, Inc.
3685 Merrick Road
Seaford, NY 11783

**Ohio**
Ferguson Van Lines
3999 Erie Avenue
Cincinnati, OH 45208

Al Walsh Moving & Storage Co.
3213 Madison Road
Cincinnati, OH 45209

**Pennsylvania**
South Hills Movers, Inc.
3132 Industrial Boulevard
Bethel Park, PA 15102

**Rhode Island**
Paul Arpin Van Lines
West Warwick Industrial Park
Box 1302
East Greenwich, RI 02818

**South Carolina**
Nilson Van & Storage
P.O. Box 3756
Columbia, SC 29230

Smith Dray Line Storage Co., Inc.
P.O. Box 2226
Greenville, SC 29602

**Virginia**
Interstate Van Lines, Inc.
5801 Rolling Road
Springfield, VA 22152

Lawrence Transportation Systems, Inc.
2727 Plantation Road NE
Roanoke, VA 24012

Newlons Transfer, Inc.
14860 Farm Creek Drive
Woodbridge, VA 22191

Student Services Moving Co., Inc.
1501 Avon Street
Charlottesville, VA 22901

**Wisconsin**
Graebel Van Lines
P.O. Box 8002
Wausau, WI 54402

Merchants Delivery Moving & Storage Co.
1215 State Street
Racine, WI 53404

# Glossary

**Accessorial charges.** Charges for accessorial services (following).

**Accessorial services.** Extra moving services that are not part of the regular transportation charge, such as packing and unpacking, custom crating, elevator or excessive-distance carry, moving bulky articles, appliance servicing, etc.

**Acknowledgment card.** If the shipper has a claim with a company, it is acknowledged with this card.

**Actual charges.** The total, complete cost of a move.

**Additional transportation charge (ATC).** An extra charge to compensate the mover when vans have to traverse congested city streets, make side trips, or operate where local labor rates are high.

**Advance charges.** Those charges incurred when the moving company has to hire outside help to perform extra services, such as preparing bulky items (pianos, pool tables, grandfather clocks) for shipment. Such charges are added to the bill of lading.

**Agent.** The representative of the van line who is allowed to act on its behalf to move household goods.

**Agreed delivery date.** A spread of dates that you and the carrier have agreed on for delivery of your household goods.

**Air ride.** A van suspension system consisting of rubber cylinders filled with compressed air.

**Air waybill.** The air-carriage equivalent of the bill of lading used for ground transport. It is a receipt for charges paid as well as a contract detailing services.

**Annual carrier's report.** A form that the Interstate Commerce Commission (ICC) requires all movers licensed to ship household goods interstate to file. It records such things as accuracy of estimates, on-time delivery rates, and speed of claims payment. When a company gives you an estimate, it is required to give you a copy of this report.

**Arbitration.** A process in which both sides in a dispute tell their stories to a person chosen to decide the case. It is a process created to avoid the time and expense of a court proceeding.

**Arbitration brochure.** A document given to you by the mover, it details whether the company uses arbitration to settle disputes.

**Arrival notice.** A notice sent by the international carrier informing shippers that their cargo has arrived and citing other relevant details.

**Auxiliary service.** Refers to using a smaller, more maneuverable vehicle to get into an area that cannot be managed by a van. For example, a road may be too narrow, a turn too sharp, or overhead structure (like a bridge or telephone wire) too low. Such service costs you extra—you pay an hourly rate plus the cost of the labor.

**Best-price estimate.** Used to describe any of a number of mover discount plans. The final cost will be either the amount of the estimate or the actual cost based on weight and services performed, whichever is lower.

**Billing weight.** In a nonbinding move, charges are based on this weight.

**Bill of lading.** The key document in a move, it can be considered your contract with the mover. It shows the total price and all services being performed, and serves as your receipt for the move.

**Binding estimate.** An estimate that a moving company gives you and that is binding on the moving company. It reflects all of the mover's charges, based on an estimate of the work to be done.

**Booking agent.** The representative of the moving company who writes the order. (This may or may not be the origin or destination agent.)

**Bottom-line discount.** An interstate discount on the entire move, except for storage, valuation, and third-party services, etc.

**Bulky article.** Term used to describe large items such as cars, boats, motorcycles, lawn mowers, sheds, grandfather clocks, or farm equipment, which usually require extra work to load.

**Carrier.** The company that moves your goods. On interstate moves, the authority to do so is granted by the ICC.

**Carrier certificate.** On an international move, the document the carrier presents to customs certifying that the goods are owned by the shipper. It is the shipper who is entitled to file for release of the cargo.

**Cash settlement.** Cash paid for lost or damaged property. Goods may also be repaired or replaced as part of the settlement.

**Claim.** Application for compensation, resulting from a loss or damage to your household goods while being transported or stored.

**Clean receipt.** Also known as a clean bill of lading, this refers to a shipment where there are no damaged or lost items.

**Common carrier.** A company empowered by the ICC to transport goods.

**Concealed damage.** A situation that describes an intact package with damaged contents.

**Consignee.** Person receiving the shipment. This may not necessarily be the shipper.

**Containerization.** Using receptacles made of anything from fiberglass to metal to ship goods in. It's commonly used with overseas shipments.

**Cube.** An area consisting of a cubic foot whose weight equals about seven pounds. Used on the estimate form to calculate weight to be shipped.

**CWT.** The abbreviation for 100 pounds. Used in calculating the weight of a shipment.

**Declared valuation.** The insurance you take on your goods; the maximum amount that you can be paid in case of loss or damage to your goods.

**Destination agent.** Agent in the destination area who can provide everything from helping to unload to furnishing information about your new neighborhood. If you want your goods to go into storage, the destination agent usually facilitates this service as well.

**Elevator carry.** An extra charge based on weight and applied when elevators are used.

**Estimate.** The household goods survey conducted by the mover to determine price; a statement of how much your move will cost. It can be binding or nonbinding.

**Estimated time of arrival (ETA).** The approximate time a shipment is expected to arrive at a destination.

**Estimated time of departure (ETD).** Approximate time when the mover will leave the origin point.

**Estimated weight.** An approximation of the weight of a shipment, calculated by multiplying estimated units (cubes) times seven pounds.

**Excessive-distance carry.** Extra charge applied when a shipment must be carried more than 75 feet (starting from the back of the truck).

**Exclusive use.** When a van is used to move only one shipper's belongings.

**Expedited service.** When a moving company offers a specific date on which your household goods will arrive, rather than a range of days. It costs extra, however. If the moving company misses the date, you will be charged standard rates.

**Extra stop.** A stop the mover makes in addition to the pickup and drop-off points. Of course, this service costs extra.

**First proviso.** Shipment of household goods.

**Flight charge.** Extra charge assessed when items must be carried beyond a certain number of steps. You then get charged by the flight.

**Freight forwarder.** A company or person who handles shipments from other companies. Some freight forwarders operating in the United States are granted authority by the ICC, but this excludes international service.

**Full value protection.** Moving insurance that offers full reimbursement for a damaged item. You get back everything you stated the item was worth (if you make a claim). No depreciation is subtracted from the worth of an item. However, you must prove the mover was liable.

**Gross weight.** Weight of a truck after loading.

**Guaranteed pickup and delivery.** Promised pickup and delivery dates. The mover pays a penalty if the dates are missed. This service usually specifies a minimum amount of weight to be shipped.

**Household Goods Carriers' Bureau.** Publishers of the tariffs of various companies.

**Household Goods Transportation Act.** The 1980 law that deregulated the moving industry.

**Independent mover.** A moving company without any affiliation to a van line or agent.

**Inquiry card.** One of four documents a carrier is required to give to the shipper, it lists the phone numbers of agents involved in the move. (The three other documents are the estimate form, the order for service, and the bill of lading.)

**Interstate Commerce Commission (ICC).** The federal agency monitoring interstate transportation. Regulating movers is just one of its responsibilities.

**Interstate move.** A move that crosses state lines.

**Intrastate move.** A move within state lines.

**Inventory form.** The record listing your household goods and their condition.

**Item 60.** A 4 percent surcharge all movers apply in addition to the line-haul charge, it covers valuation insurance costs.

**Line-haul charge.** This is the basic charge for a move. It covers the loading of goods onto the truck, transportation to the destination, and unloading.

**Long-distance move.** A move that cannot be completed in one day.

**Lump-sum value.** Valuation insurance in excess of $1.25 multiplied by the number of pounds in the shipment.

**Motor Carrier Act of 1980.** Law drafted to reduce regulation of the moving industry.

**Net weight.** Weight of a shipment, derived by subtracting the tare weight from the gross weight. The net weight is what the shipper pays for.

**Nonpeak-season rates.** Moving rates that apply from the end of September to the middle of May. They are generally 10 percent cheaper than the rates during peak months.

**Notification of delay.** Notice required by the ICC and given by the carrier to the shipper in the event of delay. The form must be presented 24 hours before the scheduled delivery date, citing the reason for the delay and specifying a new delivery date.

**110 percent collection option.** Also known as the maximum collection option, this refers to the maximum amount a shipper can collect should the final weight of a shipment be more than the original estimate. Anything over 110 percent should be paid within 30 days.

**Order for service.** A form that authorizes a moving company to transport your goods. It shows all the details of the move, including what is being shipped and what is not. Also known as the estimate/order for service.

**Origin.** The starting point of the move.

**Origin agent.** The agent who handles the estimating, scheduling, packing, and loading of the shipment. The origin agent may also be the booking agent.

**Overage.** A situation in which the shipper receives someone else's belongings (in addition to his or her own).

**Overcharge claim.** A claim asserting that the carrier's charges were greater than they should have been.

**Overseas bill of lading.** Serves the same purpose as a bill of lading for land shipments.

**Overtime.** Extra charge to the shipper for work performed by the mover outside of normal business hours (Monday through Friday, 8 A.M. to 5 P.M.). Overtime charges apply only if they result from shipper error or choice, or local laws or ordinances. If the movers work overtime of their own volition, charges do not apply.

**Owner-operators.** Truck owners who are hired by moving companies to transport goods.

**Packed by carrier.** Refers to goods packed by the mover.

**Packed by owner.** When the shipper packs his or her own goods.

**Packing date.** Date reserved for carrier packing (usually the day before the move).

**Packing list.** List of all articles in a container shipment.

**Peak-season rates.** Rates that apply from May 15 to September 30, when moving is 10 percent more expensive than it is at other (nonpeak) times of the year.

**Performance report.** Report detailing on-time delivery, claim handling, and other performance data relating to the mover, who is required to give the report to the shipper prior to moving. It is of limited value, since it is prepared by the movers themselves.

**Port-to-door.** On international moves, this service delivers goods from origin to destination.

**Port-to-port.** Service that just delivers goods from origin to the port of the country the goods will enter.

**Preferred arrival date.** The date the shipper prefers his or her goods to be delivered.

**Proviso.** Articles to be shipped are classified as commodities, and as such are either first, second, or third proviso. First refers to household goods, second to office goods, and third to anything requiring special handing, such as exhibits or displays.

**Register.** The process of providing the van line with all the moving information so it can make the necessary arrangements (assigning agents, scheduling, etc.).

**Registration number.** The number that identifies a shipment of household goods. It is used on all documents.

**Released value.** The least amount (60 cents per pound) that a shipper can be liable for. To obtain this value, the shipper must ask the carrier for it in writing.

**Released-value rate.** The rate applied when the shipper signs away carrier liability on the shipment in return for a lower transportation cost.

**Replacement cost.** The cost of replacing a piece of property that is lost or damaged.

**Reweigh.** A procedure performed free of charge by the mover when there is a question as to the accurate weight of a shipment. However, the shipper is obligated to pay charges based on the reweigh, not the original charges. The reweigh charges may be lower or higher.

**Right of recision.** Allows the shipper to cancel a contract within three days of signing it.

**Salvage.** Attempt by the carrier to recoup money for goods that were damaged in the move and for which the carrier already paid full price in a settlement.

**Scale ticket.** A ticket that states the gross or tare weight as measured by an official scale.

**Second proviso.** Goods shipped by offices, hospitals, and the like.

**Shipper.** The party (or representative) whose belongings are being moved.

**Short haul.** Shipments that travel less than 400 miles.

**Storage-in-transit (SIT).** Temporary storage of a shipment, usually because the shipper has not found a home for his or her goods. The storage period is restricted to 180 days, starting from the day the goods are picked up by the storage company.

**Table of measurements.** An individual document or part of the order for service that lists typical household goods in terms of their cubic size, which is converted to weight at the rate of seven pounds per cube to arrive at the estimated weight for a shipment.

**Tare weight.** The weight of the empty truck before loading.

**Tariff.** A list of rules and rates accepted by the ICC and published by the Household Goods Carriers' Bureau. Carriers use this list to compute moving charges.

**Third-party service.** Moving services that are provided by someone other than the carrier, agent, or driver. They might include preparing a pool table for transport or tuning a piano after delivery.

**Third proviso.** Types of goods that require special handling.

**Tracer letter.** A letter sent to all shippers moving goods on a particular van in an attempt to track down another shipper's lost goods.

**Transportation charge.** The basic charge in a move for loading and unloading goods, based on the weight of the goods and the distance transported. Valuation, packing, boxes, and the like are charged for separately.

**Valuation.** States the value you assigned to your goods and the maximum liability of the carrier.

**Van line.** A large mover that employs a mix of agents and salaried employees to make moves.

**Waiting time.** The period of time the movers spend waiting for the shipper to arrive at the destination. The more waiting time involved, the more it costs.

**Weighing procedure.** A truck weighing procedure to derive actual costs for a move. To obtain the correct weight of a shipment, the driver and movers should be off the truck, gas tanks should be full, and all moving equipment should be on board. This is called the *tare weight.* Once the truck is fully loaded with goods, the *gross weight* is determined. Tare weight is subtracted from gross weight to obtain the *net weight,* which is what the line-haul rate is based on. A certified scale must be used and must be operated by a certified weighmaster. Whenever possible, the same scale should be used for all weighings.

# Index

Added valuation, 19
Addendum form, 24
Additional transportation charges,
    21–22
Agents, 5–7
Airlines, 48–50
    shipping pets on, 41–42
American Airlines, 48
American Animal Hospital
        Association, 45
American Movers Conference, 76
American Red Ball, 18
American Society of Appraisers, 75
Amtrak, 49, 50
Animals, transporting, 41–45
Appliances, 17, 33–35
Arbitration of disputes, 76, 77
Arpin, Paul, Company, 18, 51
Atlas Van Lines International, 18, 66
Authority to move goods, 7

Beds, 36
Bekins Van Lines, 18
Best-price estimates, 22
Bids, 10, 14, 22–28
    binding, 7, 22–23, 28
    for international moves, 65
    for intrastate moves, 62
    low-ball, 24, 28
    nonbinding, 22
Billing errors, 88
Bill of lading, 85–87, 89
Boats, 37

Bonus for selling your home, 18
Books, 40
    cartons for, 30
    shipping, 47–48, 50
Boxes. See Cartons
Budget Car and Truck Rental, 52
Bulky articles, extra charges for, 17
Buses, shipping on, 49
Business accounts, canceling or
        notifying, 11

Car, transporting pets by, 42–43
Cartons, 15–16, 28, 30–31, 45
Cats. See Pets, transporting
Census Bureau, U.S., 13
Change-of-address cards, 11
Children
    appointing legal guardian for, 69
    impact of moving on, 3
Claims, filing, 71–77
Clothing, 36
    disposing of, 40–41
Complaints, checking for, 8
Consumer affairs departments, 8
Costs, 15–28
    of do-it-yourself moving, 2–3,
        51–55
    of international moves, 65
    of intrastate moves, 60, 62

Damage
    filing claim for, 71–77
    watching for, 89

Deadheading, 7
Desks, 35
Destination agents, 5, 64
Dishes, packing, 30, 34
Dishwasher, 34
Distance, costs and, 15
Dogs. See Pets, transporting
Do-it-yourself moving, 2–3, 51–57
    intrastate, 62
Dressers, 35
Dryer, 34

Electric systems, foreign, 69
Electronic equipment, 36
Elevator carry, 16–17, 28
Estimates. See Bids
Exception symbols, 72
Excessive-distance carry, 17, 28
Exclusive use of vehicle, 21
Exotic pets, 42, 44
Expedited service, 21
Extraordinary value, items of, 20, 72,
        74–77

File cabinets, 35
Financial matters for international
        moves, 69
Fish, 41, 43
Food
    cost of, on do-it-yourself moves,
        53–54
    using up, 12, 39–40
Foreign residency requirements, 67
Freight forwarder, 64

Fristoe, John W., 1
Full-replacement coverage, 19–20
Full-value protection, 19
Furniture, 35–36
   disposing of, 40
   calculating cubic footage of, 56

Garage sales, 12
Gas expenses, 53
Governmental agencies, notification
   of, 11
Gross weight, 22
Guaranteed pledge delay claim, 76
Guaranteed service, 20

Hertz Penske Truck Rental, 52
Homeowner's insurance, 75
Horses, 43–44
Hot tubs, 30
Hourly rates, 59–60, 62
Household Goods Carriers' Bureau
   (HGCB), 6, 15
Household items, using up, 12

Independent carriers, 6
Insurance, 3, 19–20
   for do-it-yourself moves, 54–55
   filing claims, 75
   for international moves, 65
   notifying agencies of move, 11
Internal Revenue Service (IRS), 21
International moves, 1, 2, 14, 63–69
   filing claims on, 77
   selection of mover for, 11
Interstate Commerce Commission
   (ICC), 1, 5, 7–9, 11, 14, 15, 23,
   37, 75
   contacting, 10, 76
Interstate moves, 1, 5, 14
Intrastate moves, 1, 5, 14, 59–62
   selection of mover for, 11
Inventory, 87
   for filing claim, 71–74, 77, 89

Lamps, 35
Last-minute chores, 85
Legal matters for international move,
   67, 69
Limited liability valuation, 19
Line-haul charges, 15, 16, 23
   surcharge on, 22
Loading and unloading, 72, 88–89
   for do-it-yourself moves, 54, 55, 57
   for international moves, 63, 66
   training for, 10, 14
Location symbols, 72
Lodging costs, 53–54

Low-ball bids, 24, 28, 62
Lump-sum valuation, 19

Magazines, 11, 40
Mail, 11
Markets, moving industry, 6
Mattress carton, 30
Mayflower Transit, 3
Microwave ovens, 36
Mirrors, 35–36
   carton for, 30
Moving companies, addresses of,
   95–97

Negotiating price, 23
New-home expenses, deductible, 21
Newspaper
   delivery, canceling, 11
   for packing, 31–32, 45
North American Van Lines, 22
Northwest Airlines, 49

Origin agents, 5
Owner-operators, 6

Packing, 2–3, 15–16, 28–45
   for international moves, 63–65
   training required for, 10
Passports, 67
Payment of bill, 88
Performance reports, 8–9
Pets, transporting, 41–45
Pianos, 40
Pictures, 35–36
Plants, 39
Plastic bags for packing, 31–32
Pool tables, 40
Possessions, disposing of, 12–13
Post office
   forwarding mail, 11
   shipping via, 47–48, 50
Private parcel carriers, 48
Professional services, notification of,
   11

Railroad, shipping on, 49
Range, 33–34
Rates, 15
Records, phonograph, 40
Refrigerator, 33
Released values, 19
Relocation services, 18
Ryder Transportation Resources, 2,
   52

Satellite dish, 36, 38
Selection of mover, 7–11
   for international moves, 65–66

Self-moving, 2–3
Shades, 35
Shipping, 47–50
Side trips, 18–19
Space reservation, 20
Special situations, 16–17
Stair carry, 16
State regulations, 60–62, 91–94
Stereos, 36
Storage charges, 20
Summer moves, 7, 14
Surcharges, 22

Table of measurements, 23–25
Tables, 35
Tape, packaging, 32
Tare weight, 22
Tariffs, 15
Tax savings, 21
Televisions, 36
Third-party services, 17
Timing of move, 7
Tools, 40
Toys, 38
Trailers, 52–53
Travel expenses, 53
Tropical fish, 41, 43
Truck rental, 51–52
Two-truck shipment, 88

U-Haul, 18, 51, 52
United Airlines, 49
United Parcel Service (UPS), 48, 50
United Van Lines, 18
Unloading. *See* Loading and unloading
Unpacking, 66–67
Utilities, 11

Valuation, 19–20, 28
   filing claims, 71–76
   for international moves, 65
Van lines, 6, 7, 14
   for longer moves, 10
Veterinarians, 44–45
Visas, 67
Voided agreements, 24
Volatile materials, 39

Wardrobe carton, 30–31
Washer, 33
Water beds, 38
Weight
   costs and, 15
   determining, 87–89
   for intrastate moves, 59, 62
Wine collections, 38–39